Ireland

Celtic History, Volume 1

History Nerds and Alastar MacTire

Published by History Nerds, 2021.

IRELAND

First edition. August 2, 2021.

ISBN: 979-8215469088

Written by History Nerds and Alastar MacTire.

Also by History Nerds

Celtic History
Ireland

Great Wars of the World
World War 1
World War 2
The Napoleonic Wars: One Shot at Glory
The Serbian Revolution: 1804-1835
Peace Won by the Saber: The Crimean War, 1853-1856
The Wars of the Roses

Irish Heroes
Grace O'Malley: The Pirate Queen of Ireland
William Butler Yeats: Nobel Prize Winning Poet
Scáthach
Finn McCool

The History of the Vikings

Vikings
Longships on Restless Seas

The Rise and Fall of Empires
Rome: The Rise and Fall

Standalone
The History of the United Kingdom
The History of Ireland
The History of America
Stalin
The Fiery Maelstrom of Freedom
The History of Scotland
Robert the Bruce
William Wallace: Scotland's Great Freedom Fighter
The History of Wales

Also by Alastar MacTire

Celtic History
Ireland

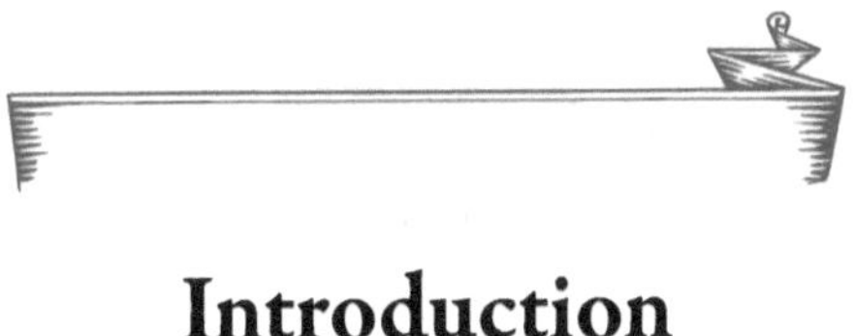

Introduction

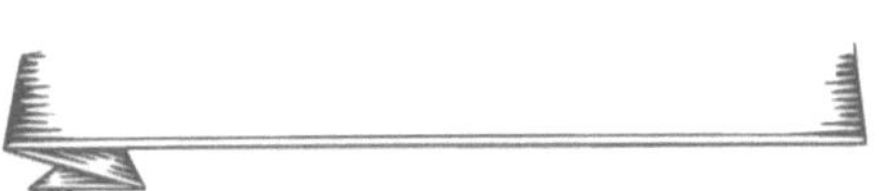

From all the Celtic nations, no-one captured the struggling ancient spirit with such surety as Ireland did. For millennia, for centuries, for decades – this steadfast drifter in the North Atlantic weathered the ups and downs, the tumultuous waves of history that battered its green and windswept shores. A country with a strong and defined identity, and with such a fierce and incorruptible heritage, Ireland stood indomitable in the face of the ages. In the broader history of Europe, this struggling nation was ever at the crossroads – its hard fate always dictated by the larger powers. As an island nation, Ireland enjoys a favorable geopolitical position, as well as an attractive climate and geography. As such, it was ever a desirable prize in the eyes of conquering powers. This fate is what placed this Celtic nation at test, and forged its people into a hardy and proud folk.

When the history of Ireland is viewed in a broader sense, one cannot help but notice that it was almost continually exposed to turbulent events, to migrations and wars, to struggle and strife – in general, to the very brunt of history's ugliest events. And even so, from all these centuries of struggle, the proud Irish identity emerged unscathed, solid and steadfast in spite of all. It is exactly *this* that defines the character of the Irish folk, that proud spark in the whole of the Celtic world.

In general, the key characteristics of the Celtic identity are perfectly captured and preserved in the Irish people. They are hardy, quick to face any obstacle and challenge, eager to prevail and to defend their own, and keen to express themselves in various art forms. Also, the Irish possess that unmistakable fibre of nostalgia, a depth of character that can only form from the collective centuries of a heritage as rich as theirs. As such, the history of Ireland boasts so many facets that are almost romantic, and with such depth that it becomes fluid and engaging storytelling – while still being firmly rooted in historic fact.

Thankfully, the history of Ireland can be observed to a very ancient time, and each step observed with surprising historical accuracy. From the earliest traces of civilization on the island, and towards the gradual development of the foundations of what was fated to become that indomitable nation. Each age of our collective history left an unmistakable imprint on that island – and each successive wave of events shaped and forged the Irish belief, culture, and worldview.

In the following book we will take measured and slow steps, observing with as much detail as possible all the epochs pertaining to the history of Ireland, delving deep into their roots, causes, and end results. Such an observation of history is a flowing work, a relaxed journey through millennia that is meant to be savored with particular care and enjoyed to the max. As such, it won't simply be focused on the Irish history at its modern core – it will glance at what came before, and what comes after, and of course, it will reflect also on all the nations that – in one way or the other – came into contact with the Irish and left their mark on that proud nation.

Particular care went towards the selection of the best and most accurate historical references: their crucial information served to assemble a book as accurate as can be. In order to tell an unbiased and captivating tale of a nation as venerable as Ireland, one needs to rely on the help of all the great authors of our time. Because, in the end, Ireland deserves that its lengthy and dramatic tale be told with care and compassion – and for the listener and reader to feel its age old plight.

The Earliest History of Ireland

Like many of the venerable nations in Europe, Ireland too has a rich and far-reaching history. What's more, it is in many ways the ideal insight into the tumultuous past of our shared world and continent – a sort of "cross section" that shows us, step by step and age by age, the shifting time periods and peoples that came and went. The first thing that needs to be addressed before we delve deeper into the matter, is the proto history of Europe itself – the so-called "Old Europe".

Marija Gimbutas, the renowned Lithuanian-American anthropologist and archeologist, left us some of the most invaluable information and theories about the most ancient history of Europe. In many ways, it is the ideal theory that brings most logic to the table. Of course, history becomes more uncertain and prone to speculation the further in time we go. Nevertheless, Gimbutas coined the term "Old Europe", focusing on the earliest, "proto" inhabitants of the continent. In her view – which is largely backed up by extensive archeological discoveries in the past few centuries – Europe was the home of a somewhat homogenous group of Neolithic cultures that shared languages, dialects, and cultural traits. This was before the proposed migrations of the *Indo-Europeans*, and the arrival of their culture and languages. Let us remind ourselves that most of us – or 90% of Europeans – speak some of the many Indo-European languages.

Still, our DNA cannot lie – many of Europe's nations, Irish too, have plenty of *haplotypes* – or genes – that are inherited from these Neolithic "Old Europeans". What this tells us is that – like always in history – the migrating Indo-Europeans mixed in with the native cultures and tribes they met. The end result is right here before us – in the mirror even! Of course, all of this intermixing and migrating was a lengthy process, sometimes taking millenia to progress. Cultures of prehistoric Europe were fluent and prone to change – religion was likely polytheistic and nature oriented, and synonymous with others within the continent. This meant that a meeting of two distinct cultures at the time was not an event of drastic and radical change, and was instead accepted more easily – and the shift was smoother.

In many regions of Europe, the oldest relics of humanity are a heritage of exactly this period – the Old Europe. The period itself is considered to have lasted from roughly 7000 BC (before Christ) all the way up to 1700 BC and the arrival of the Bronze Age. The peoples of this era were quite unique, in every aspect. This was an age of the so-called Megalithic builders, an era of *matriarchal* (a social system where women hold positions of power), peaceful societies with a pantheon centered on goddesses. These societies were likely heavily in connection with the nature and natural phenomena, and the cult of fertility was likely a main feature of their religion. Of course, this being such an archaic period of our history, it is still a subject of much speculation and controversy. Either way, there are several theories presented. One that is widely accepted is the so-called *Kurgan Hypothesis*, which tells us that the Indo-European peoples migrated from the Pontic-Caspian Steppes north of the Black Sea and into modern day Europe. According to the established theory, this occurred in a long period, systematically, between roughly 4000 BC to 1000 BC. These peoples had a different culture and a different language. Their society and culture was *patriarchal* (male oriented). They brought with them violence and war, and metallurgy, and new industries – and overwhelmed the societies of Old Europe. Their language eventually spread out into different dialects, which eventually grew into separate languages – the ones we speak today. However, whether their migration was violent or not, remains disputed.

Either way, the history of Neolithic Europe, and the identity of all of us living in it today, is one grand mix of peoples and cultures of the ancient times. With the onset of the Neolithic – the final stage of the Stone Age – people reached a new phase of their cultural and social growth. The old hunter gatherer, migratory nomadic lifestyles of the prehistory were quickly going out of fashion. New technologies appeared and spread like wildfire. This is today known as the Neolithic Revolution, a widespread shift towards agriculture, animal husbandry, and sedentary settlements. Communal life in villages and walled cities became common, and this shifted the human focus from simple survival in tune with nature – to one of social castes, prestige, and wealth. It was, in fact, the Neolithic Revolution that paved the way for humanity to reach the future it inhabits today. Migrations were commonplace, trade networks became established, and religion gained leverage. By the onset of the Copper Age, and then later Bronze and Iron Ages, the path for humanity was set in stone – and the rest is history.

The detailed view of this ancient, prehistoric period is perfectly seen in the history of Ireland. That lonesome island in the North Atlantic is somewhat like a cake – if one was to cut a slice of it, a perfect cross section of the ages would be revealed. Of course, this in no way indicates a history of leisure or a nation of malleable people. Instead, it denotes a heritage of struggle, of constant change and turmoil – of strife and perseverance. And through this history of intertwining people, of cultures new and old, and conflicts aplenty, emerged the Irish people – rich in history, rich in character, and endlessly strong.

The Arrival of the Celtic Culture

When inquiring about the general history of Ireland, many people often ask one question straight away: when did Ireland become a Celtic-speaking nation? Before we dive into this question properly, we need to remember that language is not DNA – the Celtic group of languages were at one time spread across much of Central and Western Europe, and were in use by diverse ethnogenetical groups. A simple answer is that the Irish people were settled in Ireland for at least 2,000 years before the Irish language, which spread through Ireland around 300 BC. Of course, modern history and archeology, as well as archeogenetics, are continuing to shed some very important evidence on the Irish Iron Age. Until recently, the commonly accepted – and somewhat aged – theory held that Ireland in the Iron Age was "invaded" be Celtic-speaking peoples from mainland Europe, eventually gaining a foothold amongst the native population and transforming the cultural makeup of the Island. Nevertheless, modern genetic studies are working towards the discrediting of this theory. There is a growing support for a complex hypothesis that states that the insular Celtic languages originated as a *lingua franca* of that era, used by the peoples that participated in an Atlantic-facing trade network with a center on the Iberian Peninsula. A *lingua franca* is a common term used to denote a language – or a mix of languages – which evolves as an intermediary means of communication between peoples who speak different, mutually unintelligible languages. With the Celtic culture being dominant in Central Iron Age Europe, it shouldn't be surprising to propose that both the Goidelic language, *and* the Celtic cultural aspects entered Ireland through trade and contacts with the mainland. This theory goes hand in hand with the genetic makeup of the modern Irish people, and displaces the previously held theory of a mass invasion of Celts. The latter proposition could mean any given group of Celtic language speakers and it seems quite provisional at best. It is worth remembering that the Celts were not a singular group of people, or a nationality, but rather a diverse and widespread ethno-linguistic group of numerous tribes and peoples of varying genetic heritage. Thus, it can be safely assumed that the language, from which Goidelic eventually evolved, took root in Ireland no later than 300 BC – and possibly much earlier. Over time, the language evolved and became commonly used in society, eventually ousting and then completely replacing the language previously spoken. This is greatly expanded on in the *Goidelic substrate hypothesis*, which focuses on the language spoken in Ireland before the appearance of Indo-European languages, and the possible remnants of that language in modern Irish. Scholars point out numerous words in Irish that are not Celtic in origin, and could hearken back to that ancient speech that was in use in Ireland's distant history. Amongst others, some of these words are: *gliomach* (lobster), *luis* (rowan), *cufar, cuifre* (kindness), *fafall* (feminine), *strophais* (straw), *partán* (crab), *petta* (lap-dog), *pell* (horse), *pít* (portion of food), *prapp* (rapid), *faochán* (periwinkle), *bréife* (ring, loop), *ciotóg* (left hand), *bradán* (salmon), *scadán* (herring) *acha* (duck), *sinnach* (fox), *lon* (blackbird), *dega* (beetle), *ness* (stoat), *pattu* (hare), and many others.

In summary, genetics – more precisely *archeogenetics* – is becoming a major helping hand in modern research into Ireland's heritage. This complex science helped us understand the nature of how cultures and identities formed in Iron Age Europe, and that mass migrations and replacement through extinction and assimilation are not always a viable theory or the logical course of events. In short, it is widely accepted today that the majority of modern Irish people have descended from the *Bell Beaker* settlers of the Bronze Age, or simply those who carried that culture in Ireland. When considered from a scholarly point of view, this theory bears a lot of logic with it: new and advanced cultures and technologies were readily accepted throughout human history. By the time the Iron Age began elsewhere in Europe, Ireland was still stuck in the Bronze Age and somewhat outdated. Thus it should not be surprising that its population was quick to adopt the major elements of the Celtic culture that was highly popular, widespread and established in most of Europe. In a matter of a few generations, Ireland entered the Iron Age with a wholly new cultural identity – that of the Celts. However, its genetic makeup remained largely unchanged and distinctly *Irish*.

The coming of the Iron Age was certainly marked by the rise of the Celtic culture in Europe. As mentioned above, Celts were not a singular people or a nation. Instead, they were an ethno-linguistic cultural group that managed to spread through a vast area of Europe, encompassing a number of diverse tribes that shared the same culture, lifestyles, and similar, closely related languages. Arising in central Europe, the Celts rapidly spread through much of the continent, eventually reaching the British Isles. As a cultural group, the Celts were clearly defined by their warlike nature, a unique style of art and decoration, new methods of warfare, and a deep and complex culture. Up to recently, the prevalent theory in Irish historiography stated that the Irish received their Celtic identity through an invasion of the Celts. However, this theory is quickly becoming obsolete, and a more probable theory states that the Celtic identity came through gradual cultural diffusion, as we discussed above. The Irish historian, Jonathan Bardon, sums it up quite succinctly:

> *"When did the Celts come to Ireland? A clear answer cannot be given because they do not seem to have formed a distinct race. The Celtic civilisation may have been created by a people in central Europe, but it*

*was primarily a culture - **a language and a way of life** - spread from one people to another. Archaeologists have searched in vain for evidence of dramatic invasions of Ireland, and they now prefer to think of a steady infiltration from Britain and the European mainland over the centuries."*

Nevertheless, the Iron Age is when the true Irish identity begins to take shape. The Celtic culture, language, and civilization rapidly assimilated the culture of the Bronze Age, taking some of its characteristics and merging them with the illustrious way of life of the Celts. Iron working that was introduced to Ireland was a wholly new revolution – this new metal was altogether far better than either copper or bronze, and it took the world by storm. With it, of course, arose a completely new emphasis on weaponry and a warrior culture, which was previously introduced by the migrating Indo-Europeans. Arriving in Ireland, the Celtic culture brought with it a new social caste, a new religion, a fresh worldview, the new language, long and deadly spears, supreme military tactics, and a dazzling art style. What arose in its wake was a social structure with a dominant warrior caste, with the *druids* – the Celtic religious figures – one step above them. Through such a predominant warrior culture, it is safe to say that Ireland of that time was very much tribal and organized in clans and kinships. Mountain tops and hills were still dominant in use as fortifications, and it is likely that this is the period when the Irish clan system was becoming fully fleshed out. There are also plenty of pieces of evidence of trade with both Britain and continental Europe.

Of course, the age of the Celts was equally the age of the Romans. Any extra words about the Romans will be considered as unnecessary here. But it is important to note that Ireland never came under their grasp. While neighboring Britain – as Celtic in character as was Ireland – was almost fully conquered, Ireland remained free from Roman influence, partly thanks to its position. Still, the Romans did show some curiosity in relation to this island, and it is here that the earliest written evidence of Ireland originates. These early writings are often crude, far from accurate, and should be taken with a grain of salt. Nevertheless, some curious information trickles through. For example, these classical writers of the Roman Era give us some important insight into Ireland's name, its *endonym*. Strabo, a famed Greek philosopher and geographer, calls the island *Ierne* – possibly a spelling of *Erin* (*Éirinn*) - but he however mistakenly states that it lies to the north of Britain. Pomponius Mela, Rome's earliest geographer, calls the island *Iuverna*, giving valuable details about its geography. He stated that its North Atlantic climate is unsuitable for cultivation of grain, but it is nevertheless so rich in grasslands, that cattle are quick to overgraze if left unattended. Some commentary from the Romans was, however, quite unrealistic, and much along the lines of their "barbarization" of less civilized cultures they met, So, for example, the Ancient Greek historian, *Diodorus Siculus,* writes that the tribe of *Prettanoi (Pretani – Britons)* that dwell on the island of *Iris*, are actively cannibalistic – they eat human flesh. Strabo also stated this in his own writings, saying that the inhabitants of the island have a practice of eating the flesh of their deceased fathers, considering it a great honor. Whether or not there is truth to such a claim is still debatable, and somewhat hard to piece together. The practice of eating the flesh of the deceased parents and other members of the community is well documented in some parts of the world, and is known as *endocannibalism.* There is a small chance it could have been a practice in Ireland of the time, perhaps a remnant from the earlier ages. Still, the consummation of the flesh of relatives can bring some severe mental and physical disorders, so it is highly unlikely that these claims by Strabo and Diodorus Siculus are rooted in hard fact. It could have simply been a way for these writers to demonize the "brutes" on the fringes of the Roman world. Strabo went a step further, claiming that the inhabitants of Ireland openly engage in sexual intercourse with their sisters and mothers – a claim which sounds like blatant demonization.

It was Julius Caesar who gave first solid and factual information about Ireland, or as he called it *Hibernia (Iuverna)*. He gives this information in his famed work, *"Comentarii de Bello Gallico"*, and places it correctly to the west of Britain, also saying that is roughly half its size.

Claudius Ptolemy, the celebrated Greek writer, geographer, and astronomer from Alexandria, gave a more detailed geographical account of Ireland that was unparalleled at the time. Ireland is mentioned in two of his works, and shows a good knowledge of the island and its position. In the first work, an astronomical treatise called *Almagest*, Ptolemy calls the island *Mikra Brettania (Μικρὰ Βρεττανία)* meaning *"Little Britain"*, and gives its latitudes. In the second work, his famed *Geography*, he once more gives the same (accurate) latitudes, and names it the *Prettanic* (Bretanic) island of *Iwernia (Hibernia)*, which is situated next to the neighboring *Prettanic* island called *Albion (Great Britain)*. He also names fifteen rivers, ten settlements, nine islands, six promontories, and sixteen tribes of Ireland in this work, which was at the time an unprecedented and highly accurate glimpse of that distant island. The sixteen population groups he names are, from the south to the north: *Iwernoi (Iverni), Usdiai, Brigantes, Wellaboroi, Ganganoi, Auteinoi, Magnatai, Erdinoi, Koriondoi, Manapioi, Kaukoi, Eblanoi, Woluntioi, Wenniknioi, Rhobogdioi,* and the *Darinoi*.

Still, no matter how much curiosity it sparked amongst the Romans, Ireland was never annexed by them. However, this does not have to mean that the island never came in contact with the Romans and their culture. It is likely that some Roman influence was exerted on the Iron Age inhabitants of the island, but the evidence to support this is few and far between. Of course, the first logical assumption would be that the two peoples came into contact through trade. It is no wonder that the people of Ireland often sailed back and forth towards Wales and Britain in general, so why not in Roman times too? According to several historians, it is very likely that Rome's complex trade routes encompassed Hibernia as well, after the invasion of Britain. This theory is supported by the fact that Ptolemy, in his *Geography*, delivered a highly detailed outline of Ireland, suggesting that some deeper contact had to be made. Such detailed knowledge of any land could be acquired either by military conquest or by trade. And the first one is certainly out of the question, which makes the relation between Rome and Ireland purely commercial. Of course, the best evidence is always archeology. That the Irish and the Romans came in *some* contact is clear from numerous finds across Ireland. Inland – these are very sporadic and meager. But in the coastal regions – the frequency of Roman finds increases. What this commerce consisted of is not truly known. Oxford University's renowned academic and Celtic historian, Thomas Mowbray Charles-Edwards, supports the theory that from roughly the 1st century BC and onwards, there existed a major slave trade between Ireland and Roman Britain. This fits in with both the tribal and warlike culture of Iron Age Ireland, and the manorial slave-owning economy of the Roman landholders in Britain. The warring Irish tribes could have enslaved each other, selling those enslaved to the Romans. However, this slave trade had a depopulating influence on Ireland, and could have ushered the Irish Dark Age, a period of economic and cultural stagnation on the island.

On the other hand, there is a bigger question involved here – and that is: whether the Romans ever landed in Ireland, either militarily or exploratory? Plenty of debates exist in regards to this subject, and some sporadic evidence does exist. This evidence points to possible exploratory expeditions during the time of the Italo-Gallic Roman general, *Gnaius Julius Agricola*, whose actions led to the conquest of Britain. Several locations in Ireland point towards a major Roman presence in the area. The foremost one is Drumanagh (*Droim Meánach*) a headland promontory close to the village of Loughshinny, north of Dublin. It features an Iron Age promontory fort which was excavated and revealed a wealth of Roman objects. Two Irish scholars,

Cooney Gabriel and Barry Raftery, both suggested that the fort was a major Roman base of operations, used by (or commissioned by) none other than Gnaeus Julius Agricola. While the majority of the items discovered here are of a military nature, there are no other indications that it was a place of major Roman military presence. While some suggest that it was an army base established by Agricola for an eventual conquest of Ireland that never came to fruition, others suggest that it was a major trade center that offered a contact between the Irish and Romano-British traders. For example, the renowned professor of the University College of Dublin, Michael Herity, offers the proposition that Drumanagh fort was the site of the major Irish emporium, which traded extensively with the Roman world. What meager Roman military presence might have existed at Drumanagh could suggest a means of protection for the gathering traders. More finds were discovered on the nearby Lambay Island, off the coast near Dublin, mainly a group of burials that contained wholly Roman items.

However, some still cling to the idea that Drumanagh was a Roman military base for a planned invasion of Ireland. To this end, they cite the Irish legend of *Túathal Techtmar, son of Fíachu Finnolach,* an exiled High King of Ireland who fled to Britain. The legend states that he returned from Britain at the head of an army, fighting to seize the crown back for himself. There is a possibility that the Romans lent their military support to exiled petty kings of Iron Age Ireland, in order to gain a foothold on the island and expand their influence. The Roman historian, Tacitus, mentions the fact that Agricola did indeed consider the idea of conquering Ireland, firmly stating that such a feat was possible with the use of just one legion and a number of *auxiliaries.* He also writes that Agricola was the host to an exiled *Gael* prince, and mulled over the idea to use him as a pretext to invade Ireland. These historic writings fit snugly with the legend of *Túathal Techtmar,* and this could very well be an actual event that transpired. Still, no evidence of Romans ever invading mainland Ireland exist. Nevertheless, it is likely that they supported – through military means – any one of the exiled kings of that time, perhaps in the interest of having an ally, or a puppet ruler who could help with the ever increasing Gael raids on Britain, which increased steadily when the Roman rule there became weakened.

In the end, not much is known about the Irish Iron Age. A lot of the semi-legendary history that was penned down in the Early Medieval period by the Irish monks could be the history of the final stages of prehistoric Ireland, which was passed down through generations and thus saved. Nevertheless, one major aspect of the modern Irish identity emerges in Iron Age Ireland, and that is the Irish language.

The Wonderful Irish Language

As we wrote earlier, the Irish language emerged fairly late in the history of the island's habitation. The language itself, known in Irish as *Gaeilge*, is one of the languages of the *Celtic* language family, and as such belongs to the Indo-European language group. However, it is likely not the first Indo-European language that the inhabitants of Ireland used – it is possible, according to some theories – that the preceding Bell Beaker Folk also spoke some other Indo-European language. Still, with the onset of the Iron Age and the spread of the Celtic culture across Europe, this new language took firm hold in the British Isles. As said, it is probable that the Celtic languages – or some universal, standardized form of it – was used as a *lingua franca* across much of Europe, that is, a commonly understood language used as mediation amongst different trading cultures. As such, when the Celtic culture as a whole was firmly established in Ireland, the language also gradually became widespread, common, and at last – the mother tongue. Of course, in the process it took up certain elements of the preceding tongue, and thus gained a distinct character that came to characterize the Irish language. Over time, it became one of the biggest and most indivisible aspects of the Irish identity. The Irish foremost academic and linguist, *Diarmait Mac Giolla Chríost*, put it so eloquently:

"...the fate of the Irish language and that of Ireland, its people, the land and the state, have been locked together on a shared trajectory. [...] The

Irish language tells us something about Irish society - 'who we are, what we mean, and where we are going' - but it does not tell the whole story."

In essence, once that Celtic language took root in the Iron Age, it gradually evolved into a distinctly Irish version of it. The earliest attested form of the Irish language is the so-called *Primitive Irish*, and is the oldest known form of Goidelic. It is attested from early writings known as *Ogham*, and are dated fairly late – around 3rd century AD and onwards. Still, some propose that the script originated much earlier – the noted Irish Celtic scholar, James Patrick Carney, states that it began around 1st century BC. Ogham is a unique alphabet utilizing a series of straight lines in order to produce a full sentence. As such, it was almost exclusively carved in stone, particularly onto upright *menhirs* (standing stones), which were often erected by or for high status individuals. By the 600's AD, the Primitive Irish language evolved into what is known today as Old Irish. This next phase of the Irish language is primarily attested from the margins of the church manuscripts that were written in (ecclesiastical) Latin. However, it is attested only sporadically and in the mentioned writings on the margins and in between lines. It is generally the least known form of the Irish language, although it shows some important linguistic changes occurring. Over the centuries, Irish evolved to its present form through several more linguistic phases, namely the Middle and the Early Modern Irish. As time passed, and the numerous hardships befell the nation of Ireland, one thing remained ingrained and untouched – the venerated Irish language. Through thick and thin, through hardships and toils, wars and famines, that language remained the focal point of the Irish identity, serving as an anchor and a buoy of the Irish people who were struggling amid the turbulent and restless waves of history. It is believed that the Irish language remained the main tongue in Ireland until around 1800, when it gradually began turning into a minority language. By the 1870's it was spoken mostly on the west half of the island and was usually used by the poorer class –

the rugged Irish farmers. When the dreaded *Great Famine* hit the struggling populace of Ireland, it affected a disproportionately high number of Gaelic speakers – as they were also the poorer class. This caused a major decline in the use of Gaelic, which fell out of use in favor of English. Luckily, modern times are seeing a major revival of the Irish language in Ireland – and abroad. Several regions in Ireland are known as the *Gaeltacht* regions, where the Irish language is dominant and used by people as a first language. Furthermore, it is once again recognized as the indivisible part of the Irish identity, and new efforts are made for its preservation and a new and brighter future.

The Early Medieval Period in Ireland

The shift from the late Iron Age and into the Early Medieval Period in Ireland is still somewhat obscured in modern historiography with little archeological evidence giving a substantial picture of that period. Some sporadic evidence suggests that the period from between 100 BC to 300 AD suffered a serious economic and cultural stagnation, one which was popularly dubbed *the Irish Dark Age.* Some propose that these were the effects of large scale depopulation of the island either through massive slave trade and export of slaves to Roman Britain, or through Irish tribes re-settling in Wales, Scotland, and Isle of Man. Others see this decline in massive ecological change that escalated after centuries of deforestation on the island. To that end, detailed research of pollen extracted from bogs and wetland in Ireland suggest that in the 3rd century AD there was a noticeable decrease in human impact on plant life in that area. During this sparsely documented period, the populace of Ireland was largely rural and quite dispersed. The largest settlements were the numerous ringforts that served as a communal place of protection and belonged to the higher class people. The character of Ireland during this time was likely agricultural and pastoral, with a big emphasis on raiding and clan conflicts. Slavery remained a big part of the overall economy not just in Ireland, but the British Isles as well.

From 200 AD and on, evidence shows that agriculture gained an increasingly important character, and that barley and oats were extensively cultivated. Besides this, cattle was the major driving force of the economy, and cattle heads were highly valued. This gave rise to the storied cattle raids amongst clans and kingdoms, which was an almost constant source of contention.

Of course, the Early Medieval period in Ireland is most commonly connected with Early Christianity. The first considerable literary works pertaining to Ireland came to be thanks to the spread of this religion, and much of the Irish identity we know today was solidified during this period. The story of Irish Christianity is long and complex, and shows a particular devotion to this religion – which quickly spread from Ireland to Scotland and elsewhere. What is more, Ireland was amongst the earliest nations through which Christianity spread, and that ensured a rich and lengthy Christian heritage. Christianity was introduced into Ireland sometime before the 5th century AD, which is quite early on in the general spread of this religion. It is assumed that the first contacts with Christianity came through Roman Britain, and that the religion gained some foothold on the island, although it is unknown how much. The earliest piece of evidence points to the year 430 AD, and to a Bishop named Palladius. In 431, Palladius became a bishop and was sent to minister to the *"Scots believing in Christ"*, which signifies the Irish (who were known as *Scoti* throughout history). He preached the religion in Leinster, east midlands, and Munster regions, but it is not known if he had any substantial success. Nevertheless, it is likely that these were the early seeds of stable Christian worship on the island.

Around the same time, another Christian missionary begins his work in Ireland, most likely towards the north. Known as Saint Patrick, he is considered as the *"Apostle of Ireland"* and its primary patron saint.

Saint Patrick is one of the foremost Irish historical figures, and a man that is highly responsible for a rapid spread of Christianity through the island. About the early life of Saint Patrick, little is known. When he was sixteen, Patrick was captured by a marauding group of Irish pirates, and subsequently taken to Ireland as a slave. He spent six years in captivity, doing menial labor until a chance arose for him to escape. Around this time he contemplated his faith and found a new and strong belief in Christ and God. When he found freedom, he eventually managed to reach Britain, where he had to struggle for near 30 days with a group of shipwrecked survivors. Saint Patrick eventually returned to Ireland, speaking of a vision from God that instructed him to preach the gospels to the needy Irish people. Little is known of his actual mission in Ireland, albeit it seems that he was successful in his endeavor. Christianity spread gradually over the island, and was seemingly accepted with zeal.

Here it is important to note two things. Firstly, at the time Ireland was perhaps entirely devoid of cities and villages – population was dispersed and tribal, and fortified ringforts were the largest communal settings. Secondly, Christianity was quickly spreading through Europe – not because of the faith and belief of the ruling monarchs, but because it was an effective means of centralized rule over a group of people. Pre-Christian Pagan Europe was a somewhat chaotic place: it was filled to the brim with diverse cultural groups which were almost entirely polytheistic. Tribal and warlike, this pagan Europe was extremely hard to control: Gods and Goddesses were dime a dozen, tribes counted by the hundreds, and each cultural group was territorial and stubborn. Christianity appeared as an ideal solution by the ruling high class. By introducing a monotheistic religion that emphasizes a docile and servile society, the monarchs could have centralized rule over a large nation with ease. This fact is one of the reasons why Christanity was accepted so quickly and spread like wildfire over Europe. It is also the reason why the Church and the State were so closely entwined. That being said, we can safely assume that this is the very reason why the Christian religion was quickly accepted in Pagan Ireland and spread with such enthusiasm.

Following the early missionary work, monastic Christianity was firmly established in Ireland – even more so than in some neighboring regions. By the sixth century AD, numerous monasteries and abbeys began appearing all over Ireland.

Over time, these monasteries became the centers of cultural development and knowledge, and produced many scholars, theologians, and learned men. Monasteries heralded an influx of new "trends" and cultural aspects from mainland Europe with new learning from Western Europe beginning to appear. What's more, many of the Irish monks went travelling abroad as missionaries, some reaching remote islands in the North Atlantic in search of even more inhospitable solitude, while others went as far as Italy and Germany. Those that returned to Ireland introduced new knowledge. A noted Irish monk, Saint Columba, himself a native of Donegal, went abroad in 563 AD, and crossed over to Caledonia (Scotland), and established a monastery on the rugged and inhospitable island of Iona. He and his companions began preaching Christanity amongst the Gaels and Picts of Scotland, and by the time Saint Columba died in 597, the religion spread and was established in the entire region. Other monks from Iona went on to preach Christanity in Essex, Mercia, and Northumbria further south.

The blooming of Christianity in Early Medieval Ireland yielded a veritable mini-renaissance in its culture and art. This could have been a sort of re-awakening after the so-called Irish Dark Ages we mentioned before. A new golden age of Celtic art arose in the monasteries and spread through the British Isles, where it got combined with the influences of the Pictish and Anglo-Saxon art styles. What emerged from this unison was the famous *Insular art*, a heavily celticized art style that drew upon previous, Iron Age heritage of the British Isles, especially the La Tene Celtic culture. This art style became dominant in Ireland, and was amongst the most captivating in all of Europe, thanks to its grandiose depictions, intricate and highly complex decorations, imaginative art solutions, and a superbly executed combination of differing styles. The Insular Art was most commonly observed in religious manuscripts and illuminations, which were painstakingly crafted by monks in remote monasteries. It was also common in luxury metalwork, sculptures and stone carvings, and other prestigious items. By far the most famous example of Irish Insular Art is the renowned *Book of Kells*.

Known in Irish as the *Leabhar Cheanannais*, the Book of Kells is easily one of the most important pieces of Irish national heritage, and is an unparalleled work of art. What's more, it is a clear insight into the complex soul and unmistakable Celtic tradition in the Irish identity. A vast and luxurious work, this illuminated manuscript is a defining feature of Christianity in Ireland – and the British Isles as a whole. When Insular Art is considered, the Book of Kells is easily its foremost representative. It is believed that the manuscript was created around the year 800 AD, but it was certainly a gradual and painstaking process – one in which several skilled monks were employed. Scholars agree that it was likely created in one of the Columban monasteries from the British Isles with Ireland being the most likely location. Exactly where it was created is unknown, but it was kept in the Abbey of Kells in County Meath, from which it takes its name.

A veritable masterpiece of early medieval Christian art, this manuscript contains the complete gospels of Luke, Matthew, and Mark, and a part of the Gospel of John. Lavish and luxurious, it was certainly one of the most prized items in the whole of the western Christian world. The art contained within it is certainly an iconic example of the unique mixture of Celtic, Pictish, and Anglo-Saxon influences, which itself is the definition of Insular Art. A clear indication of its luxurious origins is the wealth of colors used throughout the illumination process. These exotic pigments would have to be imported from the Mediterranean, and as far east as the area known today as Afghanistan, which stands a clear insight into the well-developed trade networks and medieval Ireland's connection with the rest of the world.

Just one glimpse at the pages of the Books of Kells is enough to showcase that unmistakable flavor of the Celtic world: the folios of this manuscript are filled beyond intricate arrangements; ancient heathen art forms mixed in with Christian symbolism; swirling spirals and endless knots; linear ornaments and a mind numbing wealth of details. Simply put – the Book of Kells is a masterpiece, through and through. To the Irish, it is one of their greatest prides and a clear mirror of their venerable, ancient soul. However, the Book of Kells was created at the height of Christianity in Ireland – at its Golden Age. It was also created at a moment in history when everything was about to change. New events were sweeping throughout Europe, their consequences echoing throughout the known world. That echo was inevitably going to reach Ireland – an island that was ever a lucrative and prized reward in the eyes of every conqueror. The name of these new conquerors? The Vikings.

Still, before we descend into the tumultuous era of the vikings, we need to devote substantial attention to the political situation in early medieval Ireland. There's plenty about this period that is somewhat murky in historical terms, and modern historiography is still largely dependent on contemporary sources , such as the numerous medieval *annals* that document the events of the era. Nevertheless, there are things that we do know. When archeology and study of historical sources are combined, a pretty clear picture of early medieval Ireland is painted.

At the time, roughly around the onset of the Viking Era, Ireland was in a somewhat difficult position politically and as a nation. It was divided into many semi-independent and feuding political entities, known as *túatha*. In Ireland, a *túath* could mean both a certain geographical territory, or a group of people that dwelt in it. A *trícha cét* (roughly translated to "thirty hundreds"), was an even smaller area and unit of land measure, comprising 100 dwellings or, roughly, 3,000 people. A *túath* thus consisted of a number of allied *trícha céta*, and therefore referred to no fewer than 6,000 people. It is most likely that a *túath* would refer to no fewer than 9,000 people. It is important to remember that around that time, Ireland was largely devoid of large towns and villages – these groups of people could be spread out around a certain area that constituted a *túath*. Moreover, most larger communal settlements were centered around monasteries, which, at the time, were centers of cultural and political power. As such, feuding Irish petty kings would often destroy one another's monasteries, causing – early on – more damage to Ireland than the invading Vikings. Some of these *túatha*, at various stages in history, would group up into confederations, ensuring mutual defence against a larger opposing force. Furthermore, each one of these *túath* had its own "army" (a dedicated defence force), an assembly, a courts system, and executives.

The so-called *Brehon Laws* of the 7th century, known in Irish as *Dlí na Féine*, contained the statutes and the contents that were used to govern these important matters in Early Medieval Ireland. They are also one of the earliest forms of law in Ireland.

Roughly around the 8th century, the society of Ireland as a whole could be considered as uniformly *Gaelic* in character, covering society, culture, and most importantly – language. As mentioned, most life was centered in sparse rural communities with a meager population. Any and all semblance of large towns or villages was centered almost exclusively around monasteries. As we know, the Christianization of Ireland began around the 5th century AD, and by the 8th, most of the island was fully converted. Still, there are some sources that nudge towards the possibility that isolated pagan communities still existed around that time. Early insights into the political picture of medieval Ireland were best described by one of the most renowned Irish scholars, historians, and Gaelic revivalists, Eoin MacNeill, who describes the five oldest political entities on the island: Ulster (*Ulaid*), Mide (*Meath*), Mumu (*Munster*), Connachta (*Connacht*) and Laigin (*Leinster*). His descriptions served as a great basis for further research into the early medieval Irish political landscape.

A more accurate picture of early Ireland consists of the following "kingdoms" or entities: Northern Uí Néill, Southern Uí Néill, Connacht, Laigin, Munster, Ulaid, and Airgíalla. These divisions consisted of numerous competing dynasties, most akin to kinships or clans. The most powerful of these was the Uí Néill dynasty, which was separated into two distinct branches - the southern and northern. Over the centuries, these dynasties and kingdoms changed their boundaries and rose and fell from prominence, and were almost perpetually in conflict. Many of the leading dynasties claimed descent from semi-legendary heroes from an Irish history that is not well documented today with many of its aspects mixing myth and fact. Either way, from this complex political picture, we can understand that the Irish suffered immensely from discord and internal conflicts. Whether or not they suffered from it culturally is not known, but it is possible that outside of monasteries, life was rather rough and centered on warfare. This could, perhaps, have been a lasting heritage from the Celtic Iron Age and its pronounced warrior culture. Either way, life in Ireland at the time was *hard*. Writing in his *Topographia Hibernica*, the Cambro-Norman historian Gerald of Wales describes Ireland and the Irish Society as *"utterly primitive and savage"*. Whether his claims were blown out of proportion is unknown, but it was clear that the Irish were in a tough spot. In a sense, they themselves were a larger threat to peace and prosperity on the island than any outside conquest. And unbeknownst to them, outside conquest was looming around the corner: the Viking Age was coming.

The Viking Age in Ireland

Ever since they managed to sail across the vast expanses of water to the west, the Vikings were a constant threat in the British Isles. Seafaring and warlike peoples from the south of Scandinavia, the Vikings were numerous and dangerous. Skilled in navigating the seas and immensely able as warriors, these northmen first came to the spotlight in the British Isles when they sacked the monastery at Lindisfarne in 793 AD. In a world that was largely Christian, the appearance of a fierce Pagan threat was unexpected. It became a sudden and violent change in Europe that shaped the future for centuries to come. Alcuin, an Anglo-Saxon monk and the man who was familiar with the ferocity of these Norsemen, wrote to the King of Northumbria, Æthelred, about their attack on Lindisfarne. His description is the perfect example of how violent of a change this was.

"Never before has such a terror appeared in Britain, as we have just suffered from a pagan people, nor was it thought possible that an incursion of this kind could be made. [...] The heathens poured out the blood of saints around the altar, and trampled on the bodies of saints in the temple of God, like dung in the streets."

The world was not prepared for the arrival of the Vikings. The British Isles – peacefully lulled to a snooze by their flourishing Christian faith – were especially vulnerable to the arrival of these violent guests. The Anglo-Saxon chronicle records how the people and the clergy experienced and saw this new threat:

"In this year fierce, foreboding omens came over the land of the Northumbrians, and the wretched people shook; there were excessive whirlwinds, lightning, and fiery dragons were seen flying in the sky. These signs were followed by great famine, and a little after those, that same year on 6th ides of January, the ravaging of wretched heathen men destroyed God's church at Lindisfarne."

And thus the Age of the Vikings was opened, ushered in by the blood stained edge of a sword. After their initial taste of the riches that were ready for taking in the British Isles, the Vikings came back in greater numbers – and at higher frequency. Sailors from ports in Denmark, Norway, and Sweden spread out fast, seeking a new life in the western islands. Contrary to the popular belief, the Vikings were not always after riches and gold – although that was their primary motive. They also sought a new beginning, lands more fertile and with better positioning. What's more, many of the lesser nobles and skilled warriors were practically forced to seek land elsewhere with mounting pressures on owning land in Scandinavia forcing them to sail westwards. Many of them had little to lose, and the prospect of raiding was increasingly attractive. Furthermore, many of the warriors were second sons which left them without the ability to inherit. These wanted to carve their own lands and riches with sword and axe. Ambitious chieftains sought to carve out new kingdoms for themselves in these islands, so they eagerly explored the North Atlantic. Soon, their presence was established in England, the Orkneys, Shetland, Isle of Man, Faroe Islands, and of course – Ireland. The Viking Age was instrumental in the formation of the Irish identity, and is a foremost part of the history of Ireland.

Early incursions of the Vikings into Ireland were generally on a small scale and rapid. The raiders would explore, find a suitable target and a landing spot, do their business, and elope from the scene of the crime. The first recorded Viking incursion into Ireland occurred in 795 AD, just two years after the raid on Lindisfarne. A group of raiders ransacked the island of Lambay, off the coast of County Dublin. Further raids were reported in 798 and 807. Of course, these attacks began the abrupt stop to the golden age of Christianity in Ireland, and all the cultural flourishing that accompanied it. What ensued during the Viking Age were two centuries of sporadic warfare and conflict that plunged Ireland and its society into another, albeit smaller, Dark Age.

At the time, Ireland was in a political situation that was quite similar to that of neighboring England. Ireland too was divided into several smaller – so-called "petty" - kingdoms and tribal policies, with just a few larger political entities that held any real power, chiefly the Kingdoms of Connaught (Connacht), and Leinster. One thing differentiated these entities from those in England. They were almost always in conflict. In fact, they were so much in conflict with one another, that their raids and attacks were far superior to those of the Vikings. To put things in perspective we can observe the period of the first 25 years of Viking activities in Ireland. During that time, 26 Viking raids were recorded on the island. However, there were 87 raids carried out by competing factions and entities of Ireland. Thus, in many regards, the Irish themselves were a bigger threat to Ireland than the invading Norsemen. Nevertheless, early medieval Ireland was characterized by a wealth of Christian monasteries – some in the island's heartland, some in the remote and inhospitable fringes. A fact that was an open invitation for the treasure-loving raiders.

By the AD 820's, Vikings increased their presence in Ireland, and shifted from raiding the outlying islands and the coastlines, to sailing the major river systems and moving further inland. Still, their progress was slow and somewhat restrained. By 832, the Vikings reached the wealthiest of Ireland's monasteries, *Armagh*, and attacked it three times in just one month. After tasting the spoils of war, the Vikings quickly increased the frequency of their raids, and the numbers of their troops. By 837, the sailing fleets were getting considerably larger, and one recorded event numbered sixty ships sailing on the rivers Liffey and

Boyne and laying waste to the surrounding landscapes. If we take into consideration that Viking ships carried between 20 and 60 men and the largest ones carried up to 100 men – a fleet of sixty ships could be seen as quite a serious threat. Either way, the arrival of the Vikings started a dark page in Ireland's tumultuous history. Just how much of an impact this invasion had on the Irish, is best seen from the medieval *Annals of St. Bertian*, which mentions, amongst other things:

"After they had been under attack from the Vikings for many years, the Irish were made tributaries to them; the Vikings have possessed themselves without opposition of all the islands round about and have settled them."

As their activities in Ireland became widespread, the Vikings were no longer mere visitors. Instead, they began to establish coastal settlements and bases of operations, as well as coastal fortresses known as *longphorts*, which were relatively easy to defend and always close to water. In time, the Vikings established several key settlements in Ireland, most famously *Dublin*. Other important settlements were Wexford, Limerick, Cork, and Waterford. All of them were coastal settlements from which the norsemen could sail inland, warring against the Irish and plundering their lands before then sailing back to the safety of their fortifications. Ireland was – sadly – a thriving hotspot for the main trade good that the Vikings dealt with: *flesh*. Slavery was in its prime during the Viking Age, and Ireland – besides the Slavic lands – was one of the foremost sources of slaves. Men and women alike were enslaved and traded with around Europe, or brought back to Scandinavia to be used as *thralls* (servants). This, combined with the fact that the Norsemen now had a permanent foothold on the island, placed the fate of the Irish people in great danger of being totally overrun by the invaders. Their identity was in danger too: over the several decades of Viking presence on the island, a group of people with a mixed Irish and Norse heritage and ethnic background emerged, which was known as the *Gall-Gaels* (Foreign Gaels).

One of the first Viking leaders that managed to establish himself in Ireland was one *Thorgest,* a Norse chieftain whose name and deeds appear in several early medieval sources. He is said to have conquered Dublin, and he is also connected with the attacks on Mide, Connacht, and Clonmacnoise church. Thorgest apparently established himself as an overlord over the Irish – at least in some of the above mentioned regions, but soon met an untimely demise. His death is the perfect testament to the freedom-loving spirit of the Irish people. He was drowned in Lough Owel by *Máel Sechnaill mac Maíl Ruanaid* (Malachy MacMulrooney), the King of Mede (Meath).

It appears that soon after the initial raiding parties into Ireland, the riches of the island attracted bigger and bigger prey. In early sources one of the leaders of the Vikings is described to have been a royal. Still, the Irish were not so easy to accept the overlordship of the Norsemen. Several early clashes with the Vikings are well documented. In 848 a Norse army was defeated at Sciath Nechtain by Ólchobar mac Cináeda of Munster and Lorcán mac Cellaig of Leinster.

However, all was not ideal in the world of the Vikings – much to the relief of the Irish. Around 849 AD, a new fleet arrived in Ireland, once more identified to be led by a "King" of the Norse. The event is recorded in the *Annals of Ulster*, which states that *"a sea-going expedition of 140 ships of the people of the king of the Foreigners (Norse) came to exercise authority over the Foreigners who were in Ireland before them and they upset all Ireland afterwards."* After that point there was a new conflict between the Vikings already established in Ireland, and those who arrived from overseas, likely to curb their rise to power and independence. What's more, the "Irish Vikings" were already becoming half-assimilated, and were acquiring the *Gall-Gael* identity. At that time, the arrival of one *Olaf* at the head of that vast new army was an unprecedented event. Olaf the White was described as the son of a King of *Lochlann (Land of the Lakes)*. Olaf's arrival remains as one of the most important moments in Irish early medieval history. In

853, this man had been accepted as the King of all the Norsemen in Ireland and had made Dublin his base of operations. It is likely that he shared this rule with his brother or kinsman, one Ímair, identified with Ivar the Boneless, and together they campaigned across the British Isles – all from Dublin. The settlement here quickly expanded from a mere *longphort* fortification, to a proper Norse town, and soon became the biggest slave trading port in the whole of Western Europe. Rulers of Dublin were styled as Kings, and thus they commanded over the Kingdom of Dublin, roughly from 853 to 1170. Nevertheless, they were becoming increasingly Gaelicized, eventually emerging as distinct Norse Gaels.

After the deaths of Kings Olaf and Ivar, their descendants were embroiled in a war of succession – as was often the case in the Viking world. However, this strife gave a chance to the Irish to make a move against the Norsemen as the conflict greatly weakened the Kingdom of Dublin. In 902 the Dublin Norsemen were expelled by an alliance of the Irish Kingdoms of Brega and Leinster. It was written that the *"pagans were driven from Ireland, and they abandoned a good deal of their ships, and escaped half dead after they had been wounded or broken."* Still, the Vikings were hard to defeat entirely. After suffering the defeat at Dublin, they expanded in search of new conquests, and were still a major threat across the British Isles, with bases in the Hebrides, Orkney, England, and the Isle of Man. Elsewhere in Ireland, the Norse presence was still significant, such as in Wexford or Waterford. Some fifteen years after their defeat at Dublin, the Vikings returned to that city, led by the descendants of Ivar the Boneless. They soon re-established their hegemony, and the Dublin Vikings became once more a *major* threat in the British Isles. By 920's, the descendants of Ivar controlled much of the Irish Sea from their major strongholds in Dublin and York. It is important to note here that this era creates a quite hazy ethnic map of the British Isles, and Ireland too. The Norsemen were often separated, with Danes being the dominant ethnicity in Viking England. And with the emergence of *Gall-Gaels*, or Norse Gaels, the picture becomes even more complicated.

Did You Know?

"The Uí Ímair dynasty arose from the Norse descendants of the famed Viking leader Ivar – who might have been the legendary Ivar the Boneless. This royal dynasty rose to power and came to rule much of the Irish Sea region from their powerbase in Dublin, extending their reach over the western coast of Scotland, the Hebrides, and parts of Northern England. This powerful ruling dynasty was of a clear Norse-Gael identity: the decades of intermixing with the Iris led to the emergence of people with both Gaelic and Norse ancestry. Famed as warriors and cunning overlords, the rulers of the Uí Ímair were the most ferocious and unyielding of all the Vikings who came to settle in the British Isles. Often compared with other great Norse dynasties in occupied lands, such as the Rurikids in Kievan Rus', the Uí Ímair left a long lasting impression in the history of Ireland, and contributed greatly to its modern identity."

The era of conflict and warfare in the British Isles did not cease. The Viking bases in Ireland were under a renewed pressure from the Irish, which resulted in the famed *Battle of Tara* in 980 AD, to the north of Dublin. It was a major turning point in the history of the Viking Age in Ireland. There, the forces of the Irish Kingdom of Meath, led by Máel Sechnaill mac Domnaill clashed with the army of the Norse Kingdom of Dublin, led by their King, Amlaíb Cuarán (Óláf Sigtryggsson). The battle took place near the sacred Hill of Tara, an ancient ceremonial burial place that was always associated with the High Kingship of Ireland. Several leading historians suggest that once this sacred site came under threat from the Dublin Vikings, the many feuding Irish families came together to defend it united. Either way, the army of Óláf Sigtryggsson suffered a terrible defeat here. Several sources suggest that his entire army was obliterated, and the defeat was a major blow for the Viking hegemony in Ireland. The Irishmen regained control over Dublin, and the Norse Kingdom of Dublin was never as powerful again as before the battle. It's political independence was never regained, much to the benefit of the Irish people. Consequently, many of the Norsemen – famed for their warrior lifestyle – gave up the sword, hanging it up for good. Instead, many took up the plough, the hammer, the fishing net and the merchant's scales – and this brought further assimilation into the Irish society and culture.

Still, their prime time was not yet over in Ireland. The Vikings were hard to root out – like wolves, once they set their eyes on a lucrative reward, little could turn them from it. The so-called second Viking Age began with the gradual return of the descendants of Ivar the Boneless into Ireland. They were never truly gone for good – they still had a significant presence in the Irish Sea, being so mobile and not dependent on permanent settlements. New fleets appeared and the Norse eventually re-established their dominance in Dublin. With their settlements at Wexford, Waterford, Limerick, and Cork, they were still a strong presence in Ireland – and one that had to be dealt with once and for all. The man to do it soon appeared on the political scene in Ireland – the famed *Brian Boru.*

Known in Irish as *Brian Bóruma mac Cennétig,* he rose to power and was one of the first to challenge both the Norse Kingdom of Dublin, and the domination of the *Uí Néill* dynasty, which held a greater part of the island under their sway. Born into the Dalcassian tribe (the Dál gCais), Brian was one of the twelve sons of King Cennétig mac Lorcáin. Remember that at the time, Ireland had over 150 Kings and a population of roughly 500,000. Many of these were petty Kings, ruling over lesser domains and being subordinate to larger kingdoms. Nevertheless, Brian Boru managed to expand the achievements of his late father, with his aims set high. Gradually, he became the King of Munster after the Battle of Belach Lechta, and soon after subdued Leinster, gaining even more power and placing the tribe of Dalcassians into a prominent position. This placed him into conflict with the High King of Ireland, Máel Sechnaill mac Domnaill, of the powerful *Uí Néill* dynasty. After gaining significant advantages after a prolonged conflict, Brian Boru was finally able to reach an agreement with the High King, who accepted his dominion over the large Southern Uí Néill province: Máel Sechnaill mac Domnaill, who lost the support of his northern kinsmen, primarily of the branches of Uí Néillm the Cenél nEógain and Cenél Conaill, accepted Brian Boru as the new High King in 1002. The following several years saw Brian fighting on several fronts: he clashed with the Vikings of the Kingdom of Dublin, with the remaining Uí Néill clansmen in the north of Ireland, and against resistance in Leinster. The whole of Brian's rise to power was one tale of struggle and hardships, and dominance won over with perseverance and that unmistakable Irish stubborn commitment to an ultimate goal. By 1013, these conflicts within Ireland intensified greatly, as Brian was now facing a major challenge in the form of attacks by King Flaithbertach Ua Néill, and then the attacks by the Dublin Norsemen led by King Sigtrygg Silkbeard. With wars on all sides, the situation in Ireland was reaching a climactic – and deafening – crescendo. It resulted in the famed Battle of Clontarf.

Taking place on April 23rd , 1014, near modern day Dublin, the battle saw Brian Boru and his forces facing a combined army of all his enemies. These included not only the Vikings of the Kingdom of Dublin and their King Sigtrygg Silkbeard, but also the Irish King of Leinster, Máel Mórda mac Murchada, as well as allied Viking armies of Sigurd Hlodvirsson from Orkney, and Brodir from the Isle of Man. The Battle of Clontarf was one of the most significant events in Irish history, and is also one of the largest clashes as well. The fierce clash lasted an entire day, and saw as much as 10,000 men dead on the field of battle. Still, at the end of the day, the Irishmen under Brian Boru emerged decisively victorious – the Vikings were utterly crushed and many of their leaders died. The Battle of Clontarf largely resulted in the end of Viking power in Ireland. Sadly, Brian Boru himself – and his son and grandson – were all slain as well. The battle has ever since been regarded as the symbol of Irish freedom from foreign domination, and Brian Boru has been hailed as a national hero. His achievements made him one of the most successful Kings in medieval Ireland and one of its famed unifiers. His deeds have been immortalized in several Norse sagas, including Orkneyinga Saga, Njal's Saga, and the lost Brian's Saga. Some however, did not fail to see the battle in a more critical light, especially in modern times. It can also be seen as a struggle for domination within Ireland, rather as a struggle for its freedom. The noted Irish historian, *Donnchadh Ó Corráin*, summed it up thus:

"The battle of Clontarf was not a struggle between the Irish and the Norse for the sovereignty of Ireland; neither was it a great national victory which broke the power of the Norse forever (long before Clontarf the Norse had become a minor political force in Irish affairs). In fact Clontarf was part of the internal struggle for sovereignty and was essentially the revolt of the Leinstermen against the dominance of Brian, a revolt in which their Norse allies played an important but secondary role."

After the death of Brian Boru, Máel Sechnaill mac Domnaill returned to his position as High King and was supported by Flaithbertach ua Néill. Nevertheless, back in Munster, internal struggle over succession almost immediately began between Brian's sons Donnchad and Tadc, and Dúngal Ua Donnchada of Eóganachta who also claimed the kingship of the province. This resulted in more conflicts and even though Donnchad was eventually victorious, the descendants of Brian Boru would not be able to make a proper claim to high kingship over Ireland until *Toirdelbach Ua Briain*. In Leinster, the defeat at Clontarf and death of the Leinster King Máel Mórda seriously weakened the Uí Dúnlainge dynasty. Their weakening opened the way for a new Uí Cheinnselaig dynasty and their dominance in the region. As far as the Vikings were considered, their threat was becoming a thing of the past – Clontarf was the last nail in their coffin in Ireland. Nevertheless, despite suffering such a major defeat at

Clontarf, Sigtrygg Silkbeard remained the ruler of Dublin until 1036 AD, when the Kingdom of Dublin Ceased to exist.

Overall, it is crucial to understand that the Vikings never fully succeeded at influencing nations and assimilating them into their own culture, but were rather assimilated by their subordinates. This happened wherever they invaded. Ireland and England are key examples, and the Kievan Rus' too – where the ruling Viking dynasties became Slavic after a few generations. In Ireland, the towns they founded became major centers of trade and later industry, flourishing economically for centuries. These towns remain important in Ireland even today. However, for the British Isles as a whole, the Vikings' impact was always modest, in cultural terms. Peter Hayes Sawyer, a renowned British historian, sums it up:

"Apart from their settlements and their influence on the language and consequently on names and on some of the terminology of law and administration, the Scandinavians do not seem to have made a distinctive mark on England."

The only remnants of the Vikings that can be observed in Ireland today are just those: certain place names, a limited amount of borrowed words and vocabulary, and certain terminology. However, the DNA might tell a different story – there could be an amount of Norse DNA permanently embedded into the genetic heritage of the people of Ireland and the British Isles as a whole. Likewise, the genes of the many Irish slaves that were led across the seas, never to return to their homeland, is also permanently embedded in parts of the world, especially Scandinavia.

Did You Know?

"The Norse heritage in Ireland was perfectly preserved in the famed Gallowglass warriors. Descended from the Gall-Gaels – the mixture of the Irish and the Norse – these elite mercenary warriors managed to preserve the exceptional warlike heritage of their Norse ancestors. Feared and famed all over Europe, they were a notorious mercenary unit that

was in use all over Europe throughout the Medieval period. Chiefly being the members of several Norse-Gaelic clans from Ireland, and some early Gallowglass families were the MacCabes, MacDonnells, and the MacSweeneys. Ruthless warriors and highly skilled in sword combat, the Gallowglass mercenaries made their fortunes in the employ of various Kings and rulers. They were the iconic symbol of medieval Ireland and the Scottish Hebrides too, and were notoriously hard to defeat in battle. It would seem that after all, the Vikings' skill in warfare was the main thing to survive even after their time had ended."

The achievements of Brian Boru ushered Ireland into a new era. The Viking Age was rapidly coming to an end in Europe, having lasted from roughly 793 AD to 1066 AD, and the political picture in Western Europe was shaping up anew. Although he died at Clontarf, Brian Boru unified Ireland to an extent, and introduced important changes into its administration. The chief of these was a change to the ancient High Kingship. After Brian Boru, the High King of Ireland would have more power and control over the whole of the country and could manage the affairs of Ireland. This was a degree of centralized rule akin to some other European kingdoms. And although internal strife continued in Ireland, the country itself was experiencing a degree of prosperity. Economy thrived as international trade grew. The aforementioned trading ports established by the Vikings were now major centers of economy for the Irish people. The Norsemen in Dublin were now no longer a threat – they retained the control of the city, but paid tribute to the Irish High King. The city was however captured in 1052 by the King of Leinster, *Diarmuit mac Maél na mBó,* who later also became High King. After his death, the descendants of Brian Boru, now the members of the prominent O'Brien dynasty, came to the throne and ruled as High Kings of Ireland. During this time, the Irish influence expanded greatly across the Irish Sea over the following decades. High King *Muircherteach Ua Briain,* of the O'Brien dynasty, brought Ireland to an entirely new level of prosperity, and he was greatly involved in foreign affairs. This rise in power and influence once more attracted the Norsemen – more particularly the Norwegians – who, led by their King, Magnus Barefoot, returned to Ireland to lead campaigns against them in 1098 and 1102. Magnus was later assassinated in 1103 in Ireland, by the Kingdom of Ulaid. It is likely that the High King Muircherteach ordered the killing himself. Still, the Irish were not content, and internal struggle ever shaped their internal affairs. Muircherteach was overthrown by the new High King, one Toirdelbach Ua Conchobhair, in 1118. Nevertheless, the reign of the new king was amongst the most prosperous in the entire history of Ireland. The nation became elevated and involved in the affairs of Europe, and it also underwent a degree of modernization. Some of the very first castles in Ireland were built during the rule of this King, bringing an entirely new aspect to warfare in Ireland, and also contributing largely to its defences. Population also grew at this time, and the high king ordered the building of a new naval base and castle, which was called *Dún Gaillimhe*. This castle grew into the modern city of Galway. Toirdelbach Ua Conchobhair (Turlough O'Connor) was one of the most renowned High Kings of Ireland, and was noted as a superb military commander. He kept firm control of Ireland and could defend it with his expanding naval forces. O'Connor also worked to create more political and commercial connections with mainland Europe – chiefly with Spain, England, and France – and this increased Ireland's reputation in Europe, and also brought more and more trade to the island. He reigned for more than 50 years – one of the longest reigns of all kings in Ireland – and would be succeeded by his own son *Ruadhrí* (Rory O'Connor). The latter was also one of the first High Kings to succeed to the throne without opposition. Nevertheless, he would not reign as long or so prosperously as did his father. For Ireland was on the brink of a new age – a new chapter in its restless history.

The period following the Battle of Clontarf in 1014 is somewhat overlooked in modern historiography, and the Irish history as a whole.

The information from this period is not as abundant as from the one before it, and it leaves plenty still to be learned. In his work, "Archeology", a respected historian, T.E. McNeill, writes:

"The 150 years before 1200 AD have been lost, between the assumptions that life was a continuation of the fifth through eighth century world and that the incursion of English lords marked a fundamental change throughout Ireland."

Thus it is that the period between 1014 and 1169 – between the Battle of Clontarf and the invasion of the Normans – received a good deal less of attention. As a period between two major historical chapters, it unjustly "fell through the crack", and remained overlooked. Ireland once more enters into the spotlight of history after 1160, when it enters a brand new chapter and a new episode that would remain etched forever in its historic heritage. And that is the invasion of the *Normans*.

The Norman Invasion of Ireland

There is a sad and major fact that we need to comprehend, and that is that Ireland never truly got the chance to experience its freedom or independence in the medieval period. This is much the fault of the internal struggles between its many kings, which also opened the doors for invading armies to seize control of the island. After finally subduing the Norsemen and entering a period of stability with a new line of High Kings, Ireland was once more facing oppression and foreign rule. This happened when the Normans set their gaze on the large swaths of land in Ireland. But before we get into this new chapter of the history of Ireland, we need to ask a fresh question: who *were* the Normans?

Well, believe it or not, the story about the Normans takes us back – yet again – to the story of the Vikings. They were everywhere, these Norsemen, and sowed their seeds in many corners of Europe. France was one of these places. During the Viking Age, marauding Viking bands harassed the coastal regions of France and posed a major threat for this nation. Eventually, following a period of conflicts and pressures, the French had to compromise, and thus allowed a group of Norsemen to settle in the northern coastal region. These Norsemen – known to the French as *Normans* – were appointed the Duchy of Normandy which in time grew and became involved in the major political affairs of France and Europe. These Norsemen were of course, assimilated in just a few generations, mixing with the native Franks and the Gallo-Romans that lived there. Nevertheless, a new and unique

Norman ethnic background emerged – although they spoke Norman French, it was markedly different and infused with Old Norse words. Their culture and character was also slightly unique. Of course, the Normans were mostly known for their skills in warfare, one of the main traits inherited from their Viking background. The Normans were known for their advances in medieval warfare, and their iconic feudal system that quickly spread over Europe. By the 1000's the Normans were a formed entity in Europe and involved in its politics and affairs. Much like their Norse ancestors, these feudal warriors were thirsty for conquest. When the chance arose for conquest they were quick to grasp it. The man to do it was the famed *William the Bastard*, later to be known as William *the Conqueror.* Quick to exploit the difficult internal affairs in neighboring England and to amass a vast army with which to sail across the English Channel his goal was to attempt to seize that nation. In his endeavor he succeeded – following the decisive Battle of Hastings in 1066, in which he defeated the Anglo-Saxon King of England, Harold Godwinson, the Norman rule of England was established. The consequences of these events were felt all across Europe: the Anglo-Saxon period in English history was brought to an abrupt end at the edge of the Norman sword. These Norse-French warriors brought a new culture with them almost entirely reshaping the English identity.

How the Normans came to Ireland is an altogether different story, and one much more simple and "accidental". Once more it has a lot to do with the Irish feuding amongst themselves. By late 1160's, the Norman rule in England was solidified for a long time. A strong manorial and feudal system was established, and one out of hundreds of Lords, Earls, and nobles was about to get a chance of a lifetime.

That man was Richard de Clare, 2nd Earl of Pembroke, and Count of Strigoil. A powerful lord, Richard came from a family that was always tasked with guarding the boundaries between Wales and England. The de Clare family was powerful in Norman England, but young Richard de Clare was not bound to experience that power for long: when he was 24 years old, he was stripped of his titles by the then King of England, Henry II Curtmantle. The reason for this punishment was Richard de Clare's allegiance to the King's rival in the years preceding his ascension to the throne. While not exiled, Richard de Clare was nevertheless stripped of his holdings and in dire need of redemption. Luck was to be on his side – or more precisely, luck met him when he met the Irish. As we know, the luck o' the Irish is known far and wide. For Richard de Clare, things changed when he met one *Diarmaid mac Murchadha* (Dermot MacMurrough), who was a deposed King of Leinster. The man was accused of abducting the wife of a rival Irish King, and for that reason he was deposed and exiled by the High King of Ireland, *Ruaidrí mac Tairrdelbach Ua Conchobair (*Rory O'Connor*)*, whom we mentioned earlier. Mac Murchadha was not about to go down so easily though, and he fled to England to seek aid from the English King Henry Curtmantle. He went on to meet the English King while he was abroad, in Aquitaine, and to parlay with him. The latter refused to aid him, but gave him freedom to return to England and to seek help from any man willing to provide it. What man better than Richard de Clare who was down on his luck. When he heard the Irishman's plea, Richard de Clare was quick to offer help. But he would do so for a hefty price: Richard would provide the army needed for Mac Murchadha to regain the Kingdom of Leinster, but the latter had to give him his eldest daughter's hand in marriage. Through that marriage, Richard de Clare would gain the right to succeed to the throne of Leinster. Some other Norman lords also agreed to help, notably Robert FitzStephen, Maurice de Prendergast, and Maurice FitzGerald. Diarmait also promised them substantial holdings in Ireland: such as the town of Wexford and some nearby territories. However, the Irish Law at the time gave him no permission to make such promises, yet he still did. Either way, the cards were set: the Normans had an open invitation into Ireland.

The first landings happened in May of 1169, when the Norman forces, led by Robert FitzStephen and Maurice de Prendergast, landed at Bannow Bay on the Southern coast of County Wexford. While their numbers were not all that high, having command over roughly 360 archers, 40 knights, and 60 men-at-arms, this force was a powerful enemy for any number of Irish warriors. Norman knights were the latest and greatest where the military in Europe was considered, and this force was one to be reckoned with. That being said, their advance through Leinster was fast. Diarmait led them, with his own force of 500 men, and set about reconquering his lost Kingdom of Leinster. First they laid siege to Wexford in early May, with the town surrendering after just two days. This was followed by extensive raiding across Leinster and even into the neighboring petty Kingdom of Ossory. Nevertheless, the High King of Ireland was soon to get involved in the conflict. Marching against Diarmait and his allies with a massive army, he forced the latter to negotiate. An agreement was soon achieved, whereby Diarmait mac Murchadha was recognized as the King of Leinster once more, but had to accept Rory O'Connor, the High King, as his overlord, and also send his Norman allies away. Even though the Normans returned to England, Diarmait mac Murchadha had bigger plans for himself: he wanted to be a High King – and now he had the means to do it: the Normans.

In 1170, the Normans came once more, and this time, Robert de Clare, known to all as "Strongbow", came himself at the head of a large army. He was preceded by a smaller force, an advance guard, led by Raymond FitzGerald. One episode from this period is recorded in history, and shows us just how brutal this period was, and how vicious the Normans could have been at times. It also tells us that medieval warfare was often – if not always – a barbaric endeavor. The story tells that Raymond FitzGerald and his advance guard were besieged by an Irish force soon after their landing. However, the Normans devised a cunning plan and sent a massive herd of cattle towards the opposing army, creating a chaotic and confusing scene. Taking advantage of the confusion they defeated the Irish, capturing around 70 men. They then proceeded to break the limbs of all captive men, and then beheaded them, before hurling their cadavers off the cliff.

Richard de Clare was no minor Norman lord. Coming from a family of powerful marcher lords, he knew how to command an army and how to achieve the goals that were best for his interests. That is why one of his initial tasks was to at once attack the port city of Waterford after arriving in Ireland. The town fell quickly after a fierce fight. Without much waiting, Richard de Clare "collected" his reward when he married Aífe, the daughter of Diarmait, soon after the town was claimed.

From here on, the Normans and the forces of Diarmait agreed to march next to Dublin and conquer it. This they managed on September 21st, 1170, following a surprise attack on the city's garrison. With Dublin conquered and with a significant force still left at their disposal, the Normans led by Strongbow proceeded to lay waste to the neighboring regions. Several monasteries and their towns were destroyed. Enraged, the High King Rory O'Connor decided to execute the hostages left to him as security by Diarmait Mac Murchadha. One of these hostages was Diarmait's son.

In a truly "surprising" turn of events, Diarmait died soon after, in 1171. It is possible that his death was spontaneous, but it is also possible that Richard de Clare somehow hastened the demise of his now father-in-law. With Diarmait dead, Richard de Clare was now the King of Leinster as was part of their deal. However, Diarmait left a son behind as well, and Irish Law recognized the son as the heir. Nevertheless, Richard de Clare was backed by that son, probably because the latter realized how powerful the Norman Lord was. Thus it was that Richard de Clare, the famed "Strongbow", managed to greatly enlarge his power and introduce the Normans into Ireland. That short episode of swift invasion was one of the major turning points in the history of Ireland. The arrival of the Normans marked the beginning of more than 800 years of direct English involvement on the island, which was to shape the future of the nation. All because of one man – Diarmait mac Murchada. In Irish historiography, he is often seen as a traitor, the King that invited the invaders into Ireland. Still, his intention was not to betray Ireland, but to regain his kingship over Leinster. Whatever the verdict, one thing was clear – the Normans now had a foothold on the island – and were there to stay.

The rest of the Irish nobles were not too eager to accept this transition though. De Clare and the other Normans soon found themselves pressured on all sides. In Dublin, the very last Norse-Gaelic King, Ascall mac Ragnaill, returned with an army to reclaim the lost city. His attack was an utter failure, and the Normans held the town. Ascall himself was captured and publicly beheaded. The Irish High King, Rory O'Connor, soon appeared as well with a massive army, besieging Norman Dublin. After two months of a gruelling siege, Strongbow de Clare was forced to negotiate. However, in true Norman fashion, he was not content with the limited propositions by O'Connor. These failed negotiations were followed by another Norman surprise: a force snuck out of Dublin and attacked the encamped Irish when they were unprepared. Many soldiers died, and Rory O'Connor was forced to withdraw his army from Dublin. The Normans held their ground.

After their initial successes, the few Norman lords that had a foothold in Ireland were now substantially powerful. Robert de Clare was the foremost of these, and had quickly become one of the most powerful nobles of Norman England. Seeking to contain the powers of his subordinates, the English King Henry II, soon arrived himself to Ireland. He knew that De Clare could likely carve out an independent Kingdom in Ireland, and that was no good to Henry. No doubt he too understood that this new course of events was a clear opportunity for him to expand his kingdom and add Ireland under his rule. In

September of 1171 he landed in Ireland with a large army and began his military expedition in Ireland. If the few Norman lords can be seen as the crows circling over the island, the King can be seen as the eagle that swooped in for the kill. Ireland was firmly in his sights – and its fate seemingly sealed. Peter Crooks, a noted historian, states that *"no less than his predecessors, Henry II was happy to add Ireland to his empire."* Adding Ireland to his already large territories would only raise his incomes and power more. Henry II landed on October 17th , 1171. This date is the very first time that a King of England had set foot on Irish soil, and marks the very beginning of the English claim to sovereignty over the island. Henry came prepared: he shipped over a substantial army of archers, knights, and men-at-arms, as well as siege weapons such as *breaching towers*. The Norman lords already in Ireland were quick to reaffirm their loyalty and to hand over all the territories they conquered. Robert de Clare was allowed to keep Leinster as a fief, while the other conquered cities were kept as crown lands.

Needless to say, the events of the Norman invasion were catastrophic for many of the Irish nobles. As such, it had a resounding effect on the history of Ireland as a whole, and its echoes were felt for generations to come. In essence, for every Norman lord and knight that gained wealth from his involvement in the invasion, an Irish lord suffered proportionately. The aristocracy in Ireland suffered the most, and many of the dynasties in the eastern half of the island were pressured and then displaced altogether. The High King, Rory O'Connor, suffered immensely as well. By 1166, he was settling to the prospects of being one of the greatest high kings that Ireland ever had – only to see all of it crumble in the wake of a brand new invasion. What started as a feud with the King of Leinster, turned into a whole new series of events that would change the course of Irish history. A pebble that turned into a landslide.

Once in Ireland, King Henry II took steps to establish himself as the overlord. He spent winter in Dublin, and there met with many of the Irish nobles. The annals state that every kingdom in Ireland submitted to Henry, except the kingdoms of Tyrone, Connacht, and Tyrconnell. The fifteen kings and chiefs that submitted to him did so because they hoped that would be enough to stave off further Norman incursions into their lands. The Irish Church also submitted to the King, giving a big advantage to Henry. The Irish clergy believed that his intervention would contribute more to the political stability in Ireland, but Henry II knew that the control of the church was one of the major aspects of controlling a conquered land. What's more, the Irish Bishops were even instructed to accept Henry as their overlord, which is recorded in the letters sent by Pope Alexander III, who ordered them to accept him or face ecclesiastical censure. Henry II was quick to organize the so-called *Synod of Cashel*, whereupon the church officials proclaimed him as their "temporal overlord". The interest that Pope Alexander III had in this was clear: by ensuring English dominion on the island, he would ensure the religious reforms within it, and that meant that the Irish nation would then pay taxes to Rome, filling the coffers of the Catholic Church. Thus it was that the intervention of the Church greatly hastened the transition and allowed Henry to better assert his power.

Around this time, King Henry II also gave the first civic charter to Dublin. It was declared a Royal City, and had all the liberties such cities enjoyed. Furthermore, the freemen of Bristol were allowed to colonise the city and settle there. In response, the Norse-Gaelic citizens of the town were forced to leave and to re-settle outside of the city walls. Their new encampment grew into a suburb known as Oxmantown, today in the city's Northside. Henry also focused on governing this new realm. To that end, he made one of his most prominent nobles, Hugh de Lacy, Lord of Ludlow, the Justiciar and Viceroy of Ireland. He also gave him leave to conquer Meath, into which De Lacy led troops and sacked Killeigh and Fore. Also, the King placed substantial garrisons into the cities of Dublin, Wexford, and Waterford, in order to protect his new lands.

Did You Know?

"The Norman Lords gained a lot from their crossing over into Ireland. Intervening into Irish politics and usurping the aristocracy was a quick way to assert dominance over the island. Of these Lords, Hugh de Lacy was the most powerful one to establish himself in Ireland. Through a programme of swift castle building and ruthless rule, de Lacy crushed all resistance to his rule of Meath. He involved himself in the affairs of the Irish aristocracy and gained more and more control over them. After marrying Rose, one of the daughters of High King Rory O'Connor, Hugh de Lacy was one step closer to becoming the High King of Ireland himself.

However, he would meet an untimely end. On July 26th, 1186, Hugh de Lacy was at Durrow in County Laois, where he was inspecting a brand new castle. He was then casually approached by an unsuspicious young man, one Gillaganinathair O Miadaig of Bregmuine, who then produced an axe from beneath his cloak and with one vicious swing beheaded Hugh de Lacy on the spot. The youth then fled and reportedly boasted of his deed to In Sinnach Ua Ceithernaig, King of Tethba, whose son was killed in battle by de Lacy some eight years prior."

After concluding the first round of "business" within his new lands, King Henry II left Ireland on April 17th , 1172, out of the port of Wexford. Some of Henry's contemporaries – not to mention those in Ireland – saw his "military intervention" in Irish internal affairs as unlawful and likened it to a conquest or an invasion. Others poetically described it as Henry's "crossing of the salt sea to invade the peaceful homesteads of Ireland" - which weren't so peaceful to start with - "causing war and confusion." The Cambro-Norman archdeacon stepped in on the side of King Henry – as was his obligation – and denied the *"vociferous complaints that the kings of England hold Ireland unlawfully."* However if one is to look at the arrival of Normans to Ireland, one cannot deny that the event was cardinal in reshaping the nation's history from the ground up. It affected the Irish politically, economically, and culturally, and – above all, it affected their independence. After Henry negotiated with High King Rory O'Connor, whereby they agreed that the former would have dominance over the eastern territories he conquered, and the latter the dominance of the rest of Ireland, the Irish people never again had dominion over the entirety of the island of Ireland. To that end, one could safely say that throughout the entire history of Ireland, its folk had to suffer the oppression and pressures from outside invaders – and never fully tasted freedom as it is, until the modern times. Nevertheless, out of that crucible of history, out of that tumultuous battlefield of the ages, emerged a hardy folk with a penchant for survival against all odds. And they kept their Irish identity alive throughout.

After King Henry II departed Ireland, he left Hugh de Lacy essentially in charge. He gave him rule over Meath – but only if he could conquer it. Hugh de Lacy didn't dawdle too much, and at once set about invading this territory. Once in Meath though, he was confronted by Tiernan O'Rourke, King of Breifne. The two leaders chose not to clash in battle, but rather resorted to negotiations on the Hill of Ward. However, after a short dispute, the men of Hugh de Lacy murdered Tiernan O'Rourke, and subsequently impaled his severed head over the gates of Dublin. Meanwhile, Richard de Clare invaded the Kingdom of Offaly and plundered the countryside. In the early months of 1173, some of the Norman lords returned home to England, where they were to aid their King in the Revolt of 1173-1174. After returning to Ireland they continued their violent expansion into its heartland. Raymond FitzGerald Le Gros proceeded to plunder and raid the Irish Kingdom of Deisi, and the latter's king submitted. In no time, the Irish and the Anglo-Normans warred on every step – no peace was to be found in Ireland. Donal Cavanagh was in conflict with Richard de Clare, while Donal O'Brian led an army against the Norman garrison at Kilkenny. Strongbow de Clare replied accordingly, and marched a vast army towards Limerick, where he met O'Brian in open battle, known as Battle of Thurles. De Clare suffered a defeat and his casualties numbered in the thousands.

The Anglo-Normans were seemingly faltering after suffering a few defeats along the way. For the first time in decades, the Irish were showing a semblance of unity aimed against their invaders. At Waterford, the Norse-Gaelic citizens rose up and defeated the city's Norman garrison of 200 men. Looking to exploit the situation, High King Rory O'Connor assembled an army from sub-kingdoms from much of Ireland, namely from Breffny, Oriel, Ulster, Connacht, Meath, and Northern Uí Néill. First they marched and destroyed castles at Trim and Duleek, before turning their attention to Dublin afterwards. However, when they saw the army of Raymond FitzGerald – some 300 archers, 100 mounted men-at-arms, and 30 knights – the Irish retreated. In 1175, the Normans used the opportunity to repair their damaged castles and from there continue to raid and plunder the regions from Athlone to Drogheda. In the process, they captured and hanged the King of Meath, Manus O'Melaghlin (Magnus Ua Máel Sechlainn). The situation refused to an end and conflict only took further toll on the already devastated land of Ireland. A solution was needed. Due to this, King Henry II and the Irish High King Rory O'Connor made a territorial agreement on October 6th, 1175, known as the Treaty of Windsor. By signing this agreement in Berkshire, the two leaders divided Ireland into two distinct spheres of influence. Rory O'Connor would be the overlord of much of western Ireland, while the Anglo-Normans would be keeping their own territories, with Henry as the overlord. Rory also swore fealty to Henry and agreed to pay tribute. While Irish sources record this treaty only briefly and somewhat optimistically, the English record it in a much different light.

However the Treaty of Windsor was only provisional, a veritable means to an end if you will. It soon fell apart, and the conflicts between the Anglo-Norman lords and the Irish continued at the same pace.

It would seem that King Henry was somewhat unwilling to control his subordinates, most likely for his own benefit, and with the aim of having larger control over Ireland. Rory O'Connor was likewise unable to control his own subordinate Kings, mostly because they were stubborn and largely independent.

The conflict continued again, and soon – in April, 1176 – an Anglo-Norman army marched out of Dublin and northwards into modern day County Armagh. Following this, the forces of Oriel and the Northern Uí Néill, under Cenél nEógain (Kinel Owen), invaded Meath, led by King Mael Sechlainn Mac Lochlainn. They destroyed the castle at Slane and forced the Anglo-Normans to abandon Galtrim, Kells, and Derrypatrick. Further attacks continued, on both sides, and several fierce battles took place over the following year. In the meantime, Robert de Clare, the famed Strongbow, died in May 1176, after suffering from an infection in his leg. Henry II then appointed Hugh de Lacy in February of 1177 as the new representative in Ireland. Eventually, with the situation with not simmering down, Henry II acted upon it. It is likely that he did *not* want the situation to simmer down, but rather saw it as a part of his plan to conquer Ireland as a whole by simply let things get out of control. So, in May of 1177, King Henry held a council at Oxford. This was an important event that marked a distinctly different policy towards Ireland. Here, he proclaimed his own son John, a boy of ten, to be the new "Lord of Ireland" (of the whole country), and planned for him to become the King of Ireland when he came of age. Furthermore, he proclaimed the territories held by the Anglo-Normans to be the new Lordship of Ireland, and a new part of his already large Angevin Empire. From that point on, Henry encouraged his Anglo-Norman lords to go on and conquer even more territories in Ireland, and expand their influence. Furthermore, the Kingdom of Desmond was granted to Robert FitzStephen and Milo de Cogan, while the Kingdom of Thomond was granted to Philip de Braose. Following this new policy, the eager

Norman lords continued their expansion through Ireland, conquering the kingdoms of Thomond, Desmond, Ulster, and Connacht.

Did You Know?

"Robert de Clare, known famously as "Strongbow", was one of the most powerful Anglo-Norman Lords during his time. Coming from an old noble family of marcher lords, Robert de Clare was ever at the forefront of all action and was an instrumental figure in shaping up the future of Ireland. The de Clare family had old roots and it spread across many generations, even after the death of Strongbow – and was well established in Ireland too. But did you know that George Washington, the First President of the United States of America, descended in part from the De Clare family? More precisely, Washington is a descendant of Richard fitz Gilbert de Clare, 3rd Lord of Clare – the man who was the uncle of Strongbow! Across generations and across centuries, through various marriages and across continents, the blood of the De Clare family reached George Washington, so far away in Colonial America!"

The rapid success of the Anglo-Normans lay in several key factors. First and foremost was their military supremacy. An average Norman knight of the time was worth several men on the opposing side. Well armoured, a Norman knight was a terrifying opponent. At their height, the Normans introduced a variety of new improvements into warfare of Medieval Europe. They popularized chainmail armor and better body protection overall, as well as their iconic long, teardrop-shaped shields. The average Norman knight was skilled with an array of weapons, most popular of which were the light sword and the light mace. The Normans were also skilled in mounted warfare – their cavalry was almost impossible to withstand in battle. Another factor of their success in Ireland was their practice of building castles. Often no larger than a simple tall tower or a fortified manor house, a Norman castle was a formidable obstacle and a great base of operations. Castles in Ireland at the time were few and far between, and not of the type that Normans built. After their entry into Ireland, the lords that crossed over rapidly erected many castles, both small and large which allowed them to hold on to the conquered territories more easily. Remember that a stone castle – no matter the size – is exceptionally hard to take in battle. Siege and starvation are the only viable means of defeating them.

Next factor in their success is the lack of unification from the Irish. Without a unified opposition, the Normans had an easier time conquering the island. This has much to do with the internal feuding amongst Ireland's many petty Kings. Lulled into their traditional customs of tribal warfare and lack of unity, the Irish could not easily get over their differences in order to repel a new and powerful enemy. This also has to do with the fact that Ireland was always just a step behind the other important trends and lifestyles of mainland Europe – due to its position. This means that the aged tribal and warlike way of life held on in Ireland for longer than it should have, perhaps due to the invasions by the Vikings. In general, it was their internal feuding that led to a rapid downfall of the Irish. When things are considered, a period of just a few years for conquering an entire nation is quite fast. That shows us that the Norman style of warfare was much like the *Blitzkrieg* of the 20th century.

Last but not least, the contributing factor for King Henry II was the Church. Having the support from Pope Alexander III and Pope Adrian IV for his intervention in Ireland, was a major assistance for Henry. What's more, many of the high Church officials in Anglo-Norman England saw it fit to exert their control over the Church of Ireland, which would help with the introduction of Gregorian Reforms. Of course, the biggest motivator for the intervention of the Pope in these matters was money. By approving of Henry's actions, the Pope ensured that Ireland would become a source of wealth for the Catholic Church. The enthusiastic Pope Alexander III was eager to bless Henry's conquest of Ireland, which has been preserved in the form of the "*Privilege of Pope Alexander III to Henry II*":

"Alexander, bishop, servant of the servants of God, to our well beloved son in Christ, the illustrious king of the English, health and apostolic benediction. Forasmuch as these grants of our predecessors which are known to have been made on reasonable grounds, are worthy to be confirmed by a permanent sanction; We, therefore, following in the footsteps of the late venerable Pope Adrian, and in expectation also of seeing the fruits of our own earnest wishes on this head, ratify and confirm the permission of the said Pope granted you in reference to the dominion of the kingdom of Ireland; (reserving to Blessed Peter and the holy Roman Church, as in England, so also in Ireland, the annual payment of one penny for every house;) to the end that the filthy practices of that land may be abolished, and the barbarous nation which is called by the Christian name, may through your clemency attain unto some decency of manners; and that when the Church of that country which has been hitherto in a disordered state, shall have been reduced to better order, that people may by your means possess for the future the reality as well as the name of the Christian profession."

Whether Ireland of that time was indeed a "barbarous nation" is doubtful, but either way, the background of this letter can be easily understood. In the end of ends, money and wealth were all that mattered in the tragic story of Ireland's downfall to the Anglo-Norman invaders. The English King needed power, and power came from territory and money. Ireland had plenty to give. One could see it as oppression; as invasion and conquest; as a torment of an innocent nation. But in the end, after all the centuries, one could also see it as simply *history* – which is often violent and without mercy.

Still, the arrival of the Normans into Ireland can be observed in a somewhat positive light as well. At the time Ireland was in dire need of technological and cultural advancements that went in line with the happenings already established in mainland Europe. Alas, these technological advancements had to come at the point of a sword, but they came nonetheless. The Normans – by then experienced in their

Feudal and Manorial social system – introduced an array of economic benefits into Ireland. First and foremost of these were agricultural changes. Their practices completely changed Ireland agriculturally. They introduced hay making on a massive scale, introduced cherries and pears and cultivated them, brought new and better breeds of sheep, and also introduced various new animals to the island. In terms of economy, the Normans placed a higher emphasis on the widespread use of coinage. While the practice was introduced into Ireland by the Vikings, it was not popular. By 1180's, the first Norman coins in Ireland were minted and in circulation. Of course, the feudal system left a mark in Ireland too – the independence of the common folk was much more curbed now. Before, they could serve more than one lord or transfer their service as they wished, but after the Normans arrived, they became unfree tenants bound to the land of a particular lord.

Needless to say, the Normans continued and emphasized the practice of building castles – which became widespread and numerous across Ireland. Round towers and fortified manors were key aspects of the feudal system on which they relied, and all aristocrats were encouraged to build them. New settlements began appearing, centered around these castles, and they began forming into new towns. From 1179 and onwards, after the program of ecclesiastic patronage that was begun by John de Courcy, more abbeys and priories were built across Ireland, solidifying the influence of the Church. All in all, the entire landscape of Ireland was swiftly changed by the Normans. One cannot argue that these changes were much more modern for the time and introduced several positive changes that boosted the economy across Ireland. Nevertheless, the ones who enjoyed these benefits were mostly the nobles – the common folk were ever at the bottom rung, and had to experience the ugliest chapters of history from the front row seats. Another positive aspect of Norman arrival to Ireland cannot be overlooked – and that is the gradual abolition of slavery. Before their arrival, slavery in Ireland was widespread, especially during the

Viking era. The Normans, after arriving into Anglo-Saxon England, recorded that over 10% of the nation's populace were slaves. Luckily, they gradually abolished this practice, especially after William the Conqueror introduced a law for preventing the sale of slaves overseas. In time, the Norman aristocracy helped with the decline of this practice. While serfs of the feudal system were still treated badly, they were not slaves. It is recorded that by 1200's, slavery in the British Isles was virtually nonexistent.

Another important fact that needs to be addressed in the summary of the story of the Anglo-Norman invasion of Ireland, is the very important terminology used in the context. While the invasion *did*, in one way, start the 800 years of English and later British hegemony on the island, the invaders of the 1100's were not English per se, even though the term appears repeatedly in many historical sources. It is crucial to remember that the men that invaded Ireland were a newly forming ethnic group that came from varied different backgrounds. The Francophone Normans that conquered the Anglo-Saxon England in 1066 became a ruling class, and gradually intertwined with the folk they conquered. Still, using the term *English* when talking about the Norman invasion of Ireland is not totally correct. There were men of Flemish, Breton, French, Cambrian, and other origins in their employ, as there were Anglo-Saxons as well. In the end, the term Anglo-Normans would be the most correct term. The wholly English nationality as we know it today was at the time in a state of evolving – from a fusion of Anglo-Saxons and Normans.

Did You Know?

"The Irish dry stout beer, Guinness, became one of the most prized brands of beer in the world. The beer is noted for its rich and flavourful taste, as well as its creamy and thick foam head. One of the secrets of its rich and unique taste is the use of malted barley and roast unmalted barley, as well as a blend of aged and fresh brew. Of course, besides being the favorite of all Irish, Guinness has a lengthy and unique history. What

*begun as a simple business of ale-brewing by the Guinness family in 1759, turned into a major success. Did you know that the Guinness brewery had its own fleet of ships, yachts, and barges? In fact, business for Guinness was so successful, that he signed an astonishing 9,000 year lease for the St. James' Gate Brewery in Dublin, on December 31st, 1759. The beer remains an unmistakable Irish icon to this very day."

The Anglo-Norman and English Expansion Through Ireland

Following the establishment of the so-called Lordship of Ireland by Henry II, a new period of Irish history begins. Ireland was reshaped in many ways – some positive, some not so much. With efficient land use, the Normans fundamentally changed the extant Gaelic society, altering the traditional ways of life in numerous ways. New tenants and settlers were imported onto the island, feudalism was introduced, and there was an immense increase of agriculture and commerce. Towns began cropping up all across the land, with walled borough towns rising around castles built by the Norman lords. Culturally, changes began appearing as well. In a sense, history repeats itself, and thus the Normans – especially those living in the furthest reaches of the island – were unmistakably *Gaelicized*, adopting Irish customs and language. Of course, they also intermarried which began shaping up a new aspect of the Irish genealogy. The Irish themselves accepted a fair amount of Norman cultural traits as well – as is only natural through several centuries of direct contact. A trajectory was now set into motion that could not be reversed – Ireland was headed towards an entirely new future. However, it has been said that Ireland, during the first three quarters of the thirteenth century produced fewer important events, and fewer great men, than in the thirty years of the century preceding.

When the Lordship of Ireland is considered, one needs to keep in mind that the government that the English King established through it was not always encompassing the entirety of Ireland. The core of this "English" government was often restricted only to the modest region around Dublin, known as "The Pale". Some provincial towns like Limerick, Waterford, Cork and Wexford, also fell under this jurisdiction. As we mentioned earlier, King Henry II named his young son John as the new Lord of Ireland. Named *John Lackland*, because he was not expected to inherit significant lands, John first came to Ireland when he came of age, in 1185. A young prince by then, he was well known for his brash and cocky attitude that is so akin to young royals. It is recorded that upon his arrival to the Irish soil, John was exceptionally rude and haughty towards the Irish lords that came to pay him homage. Subsequently, young John granted territories and titles to some of his Anglo-Norman lords. The northeastern portions of the Kingdom Of Limerick (nowadays County Tipperary), he granted to William de Burgh, Philip of Worcester, and to Theobald Walter, whom he annointed as the first hereditary Baron Butler. From these nobles important Irish families would grow in subsequent centuries.

John went on to reign as King from 1199 to 1216, and during that reign he divided the territorial grants in Ireland into smaller shares amongst a large number of tenants-in-chief. During this time, the Normans continued their policy of building castles wherever they settled, and thus they kept a strong grip on Ireland.

Did You Know?

"Hurling is one of Ireland's oldest and most famous sports. Known in Irish as "iománaíocht", the game has deep and ancient Gaelic origins, and has become an inseparable part of Irish identity over the centuries. Hurling involves the use of specially designed hurley sticks that are used to launch a small "sliotar" ball in between the goalposts of the opposing team. A complex and challenging game, it has a long recorded history, with origins rooted in Gaelic pre-Christian society. As such, it is one of the oldest sports of Europe. Did you know that in ancient times, entire villages would be involved in a single hurling match? These could go on

for several days on end before a winner would emerge. Today, Hurling is a loved sport all over the island."

It is crucial to note that the English Kings were rarely directly involved in the development of affairs in Ireland. Too busy dealing with other affairs in their realm, they only intervened when the greedy Normans in Ireland threatened to get too powerful. This means that there was no central direction to the Norman Lordship over Ireland. For example, when John de Courcy – one of the most powerful of the Anglo-Norman Lords – began gaining territories to the west of River Bann, King John promptly intervened and disinherited him, giving all his lands to Hugh de Lacy, Earl of Ulster – the son of late Hugh de Lacy of whom we talked about. John was also the instrumental figure in laying the foundations of royal government in Ireland. In fact, the origins of the modern Irish political and legal systems are firmly rooted in this period. In essence, the Justiciar of Ireland, being the representative of the King of England, would rely on the information and the advices of a council of select tenants-in-chief. After such a council, important legal matters would be resolved. Over time, this "King's Council" in Ireland evolved and took on a more serious and governmental role. It expanded and was in time assisted by a number of permanent officials who received salaries for their work. Over the course of the 13th century, these developed into Great Councils, attended by the king's officials and the nobles of Ireland in general, and soon acquired a style of the parliamentary sessions as were used at the time in England. The seat of this government in Ireland was the lavish and powerful Dublin Castle, whose construction was ordered by King John in 1204. During this period the coinage system was expanded throughout Norman Ireland, and thus the royal revenues (taxes) could be collected throughout the realm by the officials of the King's Justiciar. More legal advances appeared in Ireland over time: the liberties that the lords had were quickly curbed, and were in time replaced by the creation of separate counties known as *shires*. These counties were administered by sheriffs, itinerant justices, and courts. By 1260 there existed seven distinct counties, alongside Dublin: these were Tipperary, Kerry, Connacht, Cork, Louth, Waterford, and Limerick. In 1297, County Kildare was also added, followed by County Carlow in 1306. Needless to say, this new and elaborate system of government was necessary for a successful English rule over Ireland, and was certainly a totally different change to the old and traditional Irish system of tribal government. However, the English system was complex and drew on several important factors in order to be effective. If we consider the fact that the most educated persons at the time were members of the clergy, it should then not be surprising to know that much of the legal stuff was drawn from the Church. This started a practice of the English Kings appointing religious figures as members of both the church and the state, a practice that ensured full control over the divisions in Ireland. The last Irish archbishop of Dublin, for example, Laurence O'Toole, died in 1180, and was soon replaced by a figure appointed by the English King himself. What is more, these members of the clergy were rarely just that: besides being archbishops, they were also fulfilling roles related to the states, such as justiciars, chancellors, or treasurers.

Another important division appeared in Ireland after the arrival of the Normans, and that is an *ethnic* division. From the 1170's and onwards, the native Irish were almost exclusively referred to as the *Gaelic Irish*, or Gaoidhil. This helped distinguish them from the later emerging Anglo-Irish, and the Gaelicized Normans, who were often reserved only to the upper classes.

By 1250, the Normans had control over roughly three quarters of Ireland. Following their policies of rapid colonisation – coupled with their unmistakable greed – they made sure to colonise the very best lands on the island. These consisted mostly of the plains, coastlines, river valley regions, and other fertile places, while the rugged ones – the bogs, woods, and hills – were left to the native Irish.

In essence, it was a massive and rapid colonization of the island. And the overall well developed economy of the Normans, and the initiative of the many private individuals involved in settling, all resulted in a quick and consistent pattern of colonization. There was a military background for the original feudal grants of land, these being baronies and the *knight's fees* (measure of land given to a knight), which once taken, were protected by a castle. From these, new towns were quick to emerge which got a distinctly established and well-laid out character so uniquely to the Anglo-Normans. Where previous large settlements in Ireland usually followed the contours of the land for the streets and the city layout, the Anglo-Normans relied on a modernized, European layout of streets laid out into a grid with measured plots of land in between. This allowed for the maximum possible number of houses etc, which was crucial for the economy on which the Normans depended. However, in order for that economy and trade to successfully thrive in post-invasion Ireland, the Normans relied on bringing over settlers from across the Irish Sea. A preserved roll that lists the names of members of a Dublin merchant guild in the years following 1200, shows us clearly that the new citizens in Ireland came from various different points in England. Many of them arrived from the city of Bristol, but also from other places in England and in Wales. There were also settlers from as far as Flanders and France, who were often in employ of the Normans – not rarely as warriors. Furthermore, we can see – through the surnames of these tenants – that the Anglo-Normans "imported" into Ireland not just the officials and the knights, and the free citizens, but also a great number of artisans and peasants used to farm land. There were also cottiers and gavillers, and all other sorts of craftsmen. Of course, living amongst them were the native Irish, who sadly were no more than serfs in most cases. Called *betaghs*, these poor peasants were bound to the soil, working in the employ of their overlords. It seems that many of these Irish families lived in small, self contained communities, and thus paid their rents and taxes collectively – as a single sum. The Irish chieftains and petty kings however, did not enjoy the financial guarantees that the feudal system granted. Rather, they kept their meager territories as no more than tenants-at-will, and still had to pay an annual rent (tribute) to their Anglo-Norman overlord. Besides this, they were required to provide the said overlord with men and arms whenever the need arose.

Alas, history is seldom peaceful – and always restless. The brief period of the semblance of stability in Ireland was not to last. By the beginning of the 1300's things were slowly beginning to change. Up to that point, the Lordship of Ireland thrived in several regards, especially agriculturally. Europe at the time was experiencing a period of warmer climate known as the Medieval Warm Period, which lasted up until around 1250. Population and economy of Ireland both greatly increased, and soon after the Parliament of Ireland first sat in attendance, in 1297. This was one of the high points of the Norman presence on the island. However, soon after, the Hiberno-Normans (Irish-Normans), were about to suffer an unfortunate string of events that would halt their progress just when it was getting good. Some of these unfortunate events were internal, others external – but could not be staved off either way. Thus it was that the 14th century put a stop on their spread and their rise in power.

Amongst the very first issues was a string of rebellious attacks from oppressed Gaelic chieftains. Conflicts still persisted in certain parts of Ireland, as the tactics changed and the Irish had to adapt to fighting the Normans. The continued conflict took a toll on the Norman resources especially when the Irish conducted guerilla attacks, raided supplies and took a toll on their knights as well. In certain areas the Gaelic lords even managed to recover lost territories. Another important factor of hardship is of course the situation in which England was at the time. We need to remember that Ireland and the affairs within it were not the major issue at hand. Thus it was that both King Henry III and his successor Edward I had to deal with more pressing matters, especially in mainland Europe. This in turn meant that the nobility in Ireland could not fully rely on England's assistance in finances and manpower. In the end, all of this combined put a big strain on the Norman lords. By this time considered as Anglo-Irish, their major families now turned to war against one another. FitzGeralds, Butlers, de Birminghams and de Burghs, all clashed.

The next big obstacle for Norman period Ireland was the arrival of Edward Bruce of Scotland. Edward Bruce was the brother of the famous Scottish King, Robert the Bruce, and was sent by him to invade Ireland. The motives for this invasion are not totally clear in modern history. Some scholars propose that Robert the Bruce wanted to aid and liberate an oppressed fellow Gaelic nation; others say that the invasion was hoped to be a diversion of English resources and manpower; while others propose that Robert the Bruce simply wanted to exploit the ongoing situation and claim a piece of Ireland for himself. Either way, Edward Bruce landed in Ireland in 1315, and began his campaign there. The so-called Irish-Bruce wars, or the Bruce Campaign, were another difficult episode in the history of Ireland, and again caused a great deal of unrest and chaos. The conflict also served to once more cause a split amongst the Irish people: the English and their Lordship of Ireland were joined by those Irish lords that supported them, while Edward Bruce was joined by a vast majority of Irish kingdoms and leaders.

Bruce's war in Ireland was brief, unsuccessful, and very destructive. He managed to rally the majority of the Irish to his side and march them on a devastating path across the island. Several towns were razed and the countryside ravaged. Some of the Irish nobles managed to reclaim the lands they lost to the Normans and to keep it for good, which further affected the Anglo-Irish position – for worse. Nevertheless, Edward Bruce was defeated and killed in a climactic *Battle of Faughart* in 1318, which effectively ended his brief campaign. The Annals of Ulster mentioned him thus:

"Edward de Brus, the destroyer of Ireland in general, both Foreigners (Anglo-Normans) and Gaels, was killed by the Foreigners of Ireland by dint of fighting at Dun Delgan (Dundalk). And there were killed in his company Mac Ruaidhri, king of Insi-Gall Hebrides and Mac Domhnaill, king of Argyll, together with the slaughter of the Men of Scotland around him. And there was not done from the beginning of the world a deed that was better for the Men of Ireland than that deed. For there came death and loss of people during his time in all Ireland in general for the space of three years and a half and people undoubtedly used to eat each other throughout Ireland."

In a sense, Edward Bruce gave Irish the hope of the freedom they yearned for, but whether he was determined to deliver it we might never know. Just a year before the campaign's decisive end at Faughart, the Irish allied to Bruce, led by Donall O'Neill, elected him as their High King, hoping that it was he who would help them take off the Norman shackles. They promptly sent a letter to the Pope:

"...we have unanimously established and set him up as our king and lord in our kingdom aforesaid, for in our judgment and the common judgment of men he is pious and prudent, humble and chaste, exceedingly temperate, in all things sedate and moderate, and possessing power (God on high be praised) to snatch us mightily from the house of bondage with the help of God and our own justice, and very willing to render to everyone what is due to him of right, and above all is ready to restore entirely to the Church in Ireland the possessions and liberties.."

Alas, freedom was one step too far. Bruce's Campaign in Ireland eventually brought more difficulties than good. In the end, the destructive nature of this brief war started a "domino effect" across Ireland that would have many far-reaching consequences. At the time, Europe was suffering from a particularly bad famine, known in history as the *Great Famine of 1315-1317*. It was caused by a widespread failure of crops that took on an enormous scale and led to countless deaths. Sadly, it spread to Ireland too. As the campaign of Edward Bruce was so destructive, it caused massive destruction of crops throughout the country. This, and the fact that the Irish ports could not import crops from elsewhere in Europe, led to a catastrophic famine that decimated Ireland's populace.

The island didn't even begin to recover from the effects of the early 1300's when another disaster struck – this time far more ravaging. Known as the *Black Death*, this vicious plague swept across Europe causing a number of deaths never before experienced in history. It reached Ireland in 1348 and swiftly ravaged the island. Some sources state that Dublin and Drogheda were entirely depopulated in a matter of weeks. With the onset of that Bubonic Plague, the island was consumed by panic and death. During this time, the picture of Ireland turned into one of pain, misery, and continuous hardship. Clans feuded between themselves, notably the Burkes and the O'Connors, lands lay ravaged, and death was prevalent. Nevertheless, this contributed to the resurgence of Gaelic power, and a gradual prevalence of the Irish identity. The Anglo-Normans were now on the defensive. This period became known as the Gaelic revival.

Did You Know?

"The Black Death was one of the most gruesome catastrophes in world's history, unleashing a wave of death across Europe that would have unparalleled consequences. "One citizen avoided another," history records, "and hardly any neighbour troubled about others, relatives never or hardly ever visited each other. Moreover, such terror was struck into the hearts of men and women by this calamity, that brother abandoned brother, and the uncle his nephew, and the sister her brother, and very often the wife her husband. What is even worse and nearly incredible is that fathers and mothers refused to see and tend their children, as if they had not been theirs." The Black Death first arrived in Ireland with the trade ships that arrived on it's east coast in July 1348. Its effects were devastating. In combination with the warfare and lawlessness that

ensued, the Plague reduced Ireland's population from roughly 2.7 million to just 1.7 million."

This period was a time of intense Gaelicization of the Anglo-Irish peoples. It is important to note that over the centuries, those Normans that settled gradually became assimilated into the Gaelic society. They still remained distinctly "English" so to speak, being called the Anglo-Irish, but now in the late 1300's, they were becoming increasingly Irish. This was especially noticeable outside of the "Pale", as the Norman lords fully adopted the use of Irish Language, and the use of their customs and traditions. Certain historians dubbed them "more Irish than the Irish themselves". The English government in Dublin was so concerned about losing their folk to Gaelicization, that they created the so-called Statutes of Kilkenny in 1367, which banned those people of English descent from using the Irish language, marrying Irish people, or wearing distinctly Irish clothes. Nevertheless, these regulations were not very efficient, and the "Pale" - that is the Dublin government – had little authority. In fact, throughout the 1400's this authority steadily diminished, especially due to the fact that England was involved in the Hundred Years' War and the subsequent Wars of the Roses. As a result of this, England's direct involvement in affairs in Ireland were greatly reduced. The English Kings kept their constitutional authority over the Lordship of Ireland through the powerful Earls FitzGerald of Kildare. They held the power in balance by effective military force and alliances with Irish lords and clans.

By the year 1500, the administrative area known as the "Pale", was reduced only to a meager territory around Dublin. The Irish internal affairs and politics developed largely on their own, without a major influence from the English crown. One of the last of the so-called "Old Gaelic Order", the powerful clans O'Donnell and O'Neill, once more became the major players in Ireland, gaining considerable power in the land. Most of the other clans remained – in theory – loyal to the English crown, but still relied on the old Gaelic system of mutual alliances. Things were about to change considerably when a rebellion arose that was to shake the very foundations of late 1500's Ireland.

The so-called Kildare Rebellion of 1534, stirred up by the 10th Earl of Kildare, Thomas FitzGerald. Suspecting that his father had been executed in the Tower of London, and that the same fate awaited him, young Thomas FitzGerald – acting as the Lord Deputy of Ireland – gathered a force of roughly 140 Gallowglass mercenaries, and publicly renounced his allegiance to the English King, Henry VIII. Alas, his rebellion was brief and very unfortunate. It was quickly quelled by the English, and Silken Thomas FitzGerald – gaining the nickname "Silken" from the silk ribbons of his men – was captured along with his uncles. They were then hanged, beheaded, and quartered. However, their rebellion had lasting consequences, and Henry VIII meant to implement new changes, and to reconquer Ireland and put it under the control of the crown. He feared that failing to do so will leave more room for future rebellions, which could lead to the eventual loss of the island. With the FitzGeralds – the Lord Deputies of Ireland – now exterminated, Henry needed to find a replacement for that position and to ensure that Ireland is controlled. The King was in dire need of a new plan, a fresh new policy that would be cost-effective, and that would ensure that the "Pale" region was protected and remain as a guaranteed protection of England's western flank, i.e. the western shores. The main assistance in creation of this plan was Thomas Cromwell. With his help, Henry VIII created the so-called policy of surrender and regrant. What did this mean? Surrender and regrant policy meant that the royal protection – the protection of the English crown – now extended to the whole of Ireland's elite, without regard to their ethnicity. In return for this, the whole of Ireland was expected to obey the laws of the central government. All Irish Lords were expected to surrender their lands to the English Crown, only to immediately receive them back through a Royal Charter. The basic intention of this policy was a way to assimilate the Gaelic and Gaelicized upper class of Ireland – more faster and efficiently. It was also an ideal way to make them more loyal to the English Crown. In no time, the Irish Lords were granted English titles, and were admitted – for the first time ever – to the Irish Parliament. Henry VIII himself described the new policies as "political drifts and amiable persuasions". In practice however, the Irish continued much as they carried on before, although accepting the new policies and privileges they got. But in the end, things were not so simple. Under Henry VIII, the Tudors gained a lot more centralized rule, and encroached ever more on Irish autonomy by developing a centralized state and an English system that conflicted with the traditional Gaelic way of life. This was followed by the Religious Reformations of Henry VIII – similar to those that were ongoing in England – and they caused some disquiet in Ireland. However, this disquiet was somewhat successfully put down with the new Lord Deputy, Anthony St. Leger, buying off those Irish nobles that were opposed to the reformation by granting them new lands – those that were confiscated from the monasteries. Up to then, the English monarchs were ever known as "Lords of Ireland", but Henry VIII was keen on changing that – and exerting greater control of Ireland. To that end, the "Crown of Ireland Act" was passed on by the Irish Parliament in 1542, thereby granting Henry VIII – and his successors - the title of *King of Ireland*. The land was with that established as the Kingdom of Ireland and would exist in that form until 1800. In order to provide better security on the island, Henry established the Royal Irish Army, or *"army in Ireland"*. For a greater part of the existence of this army – which was until 1801 – only the Prostestant Anglo-Irish could join its ranks.

Did You Know?

"William Butler Yeats (13 June 1865 – 28 January 1939), was one of the most renowned Irish poets and dramatists, and also one of the most renowned in the world. One of the foremost figures in the Irish literary establishment, Yeats' talent and work helped him become one of the

celebrated figures of 20th century literature. Written in true Irish style and embodying the iconic Irish spirit, the poems of William Butler Yeats continue to inspire countless souls, and to be extensively studied around the world. A proud Irishman, Yeats also served two terms as a Senator for the Irish Free State. In 1923, he received a Nobel Prize for Literature, bringing Irish poetry and writing much deserved recognition and placing it at an all time high popularity. Poignant, romantic, and at times patriotic, his poetry continues to be a fiercely burning flame of Irish national heritage."

Protestant Settlement and the Changing Fate of Ireland

The settlement of protestants in Ireland during the reign of Elizabeth I (the second daughter of Henry VIII) gained even wider proportions, and covered the period from 1558 to 1603. After crossing the "Pale" area, Protestants saw that people in Ireland, of all ethnicities, lived a different way of life than back home in England. Queen Elizabeth, who first and foremost sought security, sent English investors (adventurers) to Ireland. Elizabethan cartography shows ignorance of the Irish terrain, as there was no real map of the Donegal coast until 1602-1603. For the native Irish, the literal presentation of their country was less important than its poetic dimension, and each place had its own legend and identity. The Elizabethan soldiers hated the landscape of Ireland. Arable land in each of the districts was vaguely defined, and the existing maps represented the identity of the dominant families in certain key locations. The mobility of the Irish through river valleys, swamps and dense forests surprised the English. The dense woods of Ireland, covering an eighth of the island, were increasingly exploited, especially in places where the Irish hid. The land was thus cleared for new settlement. Wood played a big role in the economy, which was reflected in the production of wooden pipes, barrels and the construction of ships. Even the nature of the separate provinces changed and became increasingly insecure.

At the start of the 1600's, Ulster was synonymous with wilderness; untamed, separated by nature and geography, under-populated, economically under-developed and least urbanized. On the other hand, in the late Middle Ages, the western province of Connacht became an absolute contrast, being characterized by economic activity and cultural vitality. However, in the years to come, both of these stereotypes would be reversed thanks to administrative conquest and plantation done by the English. Other areas such as Armagh and Antrim were already familiar for their rural landscapes with familiar patterns as well as the construction of large luxury residences of the Anglo-Irish aristocracy. In Munster, Richard Boyle, an ambitious planter, tried to shape the landscape after the English fashion: a manor house, surrounded by a deer park, selected orchards, fish ponds, horse farms, and meticulously developed rabbit habitats as was the ideal example of traditionally English manor-land. The idea was to create a flourishing English "garden", even in the wildest reaches of Ireland. It was another important factor in creating a new face of Ireland - as equally as crucial as the increase in logging, building of castles and manors, an increase in towns, smelting of iron, and building of homes for the poorest classes in Ireland. The structure of the landscapes reflected the incompleteness of the conquest, and that perception can be understood from the witnesses of the era, whose writings created a picture of Elizabethan Ireland for their contemporaries. Writers such as Edmund Spenser, who wrote in his major work, "The View of the Present State of Ireland", paint a stark picture of the island, mentioning how the Elizabethan Englishmen believed that the "Irish nationality could only be eradicated by the sword." The Elizabethan conquest of Ireland was to be the birth of a new, flourishing Irish civilization. However, to fully reshape Ireland, the old Gaelic lifestyle had to be changed as well. In Ireland, priests enjoyed a big reputation amongst the people, but the true social influence was in other hands altogether - the elites. Priests of the European Counter Reformation, which was active in Ireland even before the 1600's, formed a somewhat unrecognizable form of Catholicism. The society was formed on the basis of the medieval Irish district (tuath), which were tribal, kinship-related units of land measure. According to the old Gaelic law of inheritance (tanistry), the heir could be determined for the life of the chief or Lord, and the heir did not necessarily have to be the eldest son, but the one who deserved it the most or was the wisest of the male close relatives of the chief. What bothered the English were the undefined social foundations of property and authority that were redefined with the advent of each new generation. The English often characterized such a reality as anarchy. In Ulster, which was the most Irish of all the provinces, the great lords, the Gaelic and the English, faced the dilemma of accepting the subjugation by the Protestants. Supporting initially the Elizabethan project of adopting English laws, English systems of administration and maintenance of property, the head of the Irish dynasty O'Neill, Hugh O'Neill of Tyrone, in a desire to preserve the power of his family, changed his attitude, and made enemies of the English, rising up against their invasion of Ireland. In 1595, he united with the Chief of the O'Donnell family, Hugh Roe O'Donnell of Tyrconnell, and started a war against the English crown. The ensuing conflict was known as the Nine Years' War, and marked an important episode in Irish history. Their struggle will be characterized as a struggle for the faith and the land of their ancestors and will later emerge as an important link between religion and Irish identity.

With the help of King Philip III in 1601, the Spanish fleet landed on Kinsale. However, landing on the wrong part of the Irish coast resulted in the loss of the battle. For the Spaniards it was a complete fiasco, and England saved its colony. Since the war was extremely expensive, it almost brought the crown to bankruptcy, and for the Irish, the Battle of Kinsale broke Gaelic power forever. In 1607, O'Neill and O'Donnell left Ireland with their families forever, fleeing to mainland Europe. This was known as the *Flight of the Earls*, and marked the end of the Gaelic Old Order. The peasants, left behind, had to make peace with their new masters, but they still wondered if the Earls would return and drive the people into rebellion. England, on the other hand, was left with the feeling that Catholic Ireland would forever remain a threat, and if Ireland could not make itself loyal, an entire Protestant order would be inhabited and determined to remain.

The largest wave of immigrants into Ulster happened in 1608 and led to the confiscation of property from Irish nobles, and already in this period the problem of Ireland and Ulster gained a colonial and economic dimension. Problems of England's economic and political domination over Ireland, England tried to solve through Protestant immigrants. The source of the current situation in Northern Ireland is reflected in the then conflicting parties: the Catholics and the Protestants, that is, the Anglo-Irish conquerors and the English colonizers. The further course of historical events will only deepen the schism that is present and inherent in modern Ulster, which will be discussed later. King James I took more radical measures to address the issue of the unstable situation in Ulster by settling large numbers of Protestants on the land of the exiled Gallic Earls. Ulster was subdivided and only a quarter of the population remained in the hands of Catholics. Londonderry became a Protestant "citadel", where the identity of the Protestants was created, and the tone of the aristocratic motive was economic power, the interests of enrichment. The Scots, that is, the Presbyterians, also inhabited Ireland and resisted Catholicism. During the reign of Charles I, Ulster would feel the effects of the rage from those who had taken the country, as England was preoccupied with civil war. The Irish turned against Protestant plantationists, deepening the conflict. However, after the death of Charles I in 1649, Oliver Cromwell came to Ireland as an army commander with an open philosophy forbidding his followers to "spare all those who could bear arms". By the decree of 1652, the English Parliament adopted a radical document (Settlement of Ireland), where Catholics emigrated to the poor and desolate parts of the island of

Ireland. To this day, Cromwell's atrocities against the Catholic population remain remembered.

During the reign of James II, Protestants, mostly English and Scots, including some families of Irish descent, owned almost all of the country, and ran almost all businesses, filled government and judicial positions, as well as jobs in the army and navy. Their behavior, customs and spoken language was English. Beneath them, unconnected to them by any threads of history, culture, or common interest, speaking Gaelic Irish, the language of their ancestors, and not English, the language of their conquerors, were Catholics, a repressed, subjugated people without rights, living in poverty, even poorer from the majority of peasants living in Europe at the time. The unpopular rule of King James II as a Catholic in Protestant England conditioned his appeal for help to King Louis XIV of France. Due to the counter-reformation that took place in 1672 in Paris, where the most massive religious massacres, starvation and terror known to Europe were conducted, combined with the arrival of King James into Ireland and the conquest of Dublin and Londonderry, meant a significant rebirth of hope for the Catholic population in Ireland. Protestants of England, supporting William of Orange, fearing the terrifying rise of the Catholic faith, clashed with King James at the River Boyne in 1690.

Did You Know?

"The Battle of the Boyne (Cath na Bóinne) was one of the major battles in Irish history, fought in 1690 between the forces of the deposed King James II of England and Ireland, VII of Scotland, against the forces of King William III who, with his wife Queen Mary II (his cousin and James's daughter), had acceded to the Crowns of England and Scotland in 1689. The battle took place across the River Boyne close to the town of Drogheda in the Kingdom of Ireland, and resulted in a decisive victory for William III. The battle was a major turn of events and caused James's attempt to regain the British crown to fail, and ultimately aided in ensuring the continued Protestant ascendancy in Ireland. In the Battle of

the Boyne, William's forces defeated James's army which consisted mostly of raw recruits. Although the Williamite War in Ireland continued until October 1691, James fled to France after the Boyne, never to return."

By the end of the Williamite Wars waged by William, the Catholic elite in Ireland had been exiled, killed, or did not fight back. The inhabitants who had fought against Elizabeth and Cromwell decades earlier were completely defeated, and were replaced by a new ruling class - the Protestant denomination (ascendancy) which identified itself as the only Irish nation.

To be a member of this class meant to be privileged, and to be privileged was to be either a born Protestant or to be from a Catholic family who converted to the Protestant faith at the right time. The country developed, buildings, new roads and canals were built, and Dublin became the capital and a major commercial city, a city of enlightenment. England had already shown its jealousy of Ireland with the Livestock Import Act and the Foreign Goods Import Act, and in 1696 England banned Ireland from importing goods directly from America, deciding that ships must dock and leave British ports, thus paying duties to the British customs and filling the British vault. By the time such goods reached Ireland, they were very expensive. England also attacked the Irish wool industry and banned the export of cattle to any country other than England - Ireland must always be poorer than England. Jonathan Swift, a famous English satirist of the time, was neither a liberal nor a Democrat, but a Protestant who supported Protestant denomination but not its cruelty, and believed in the indisputable right of Protestants to rule Ireland. In his work *"A Proposal for the Universal Use of Irish Manufacture"* he describes the misery of the laundress, and in Drapeir's Letters he says of the Irish, *"By the law of God, the law of nature, the people, and your own country, you are and must be a free people, like your English brothers."*

Ever since the enactment of the fourteenth century Kilkenny Statutes, which were also based on religious discrimination, the appointment of Protestants as the ruling class has caused Catholicism to be equated with nationalism. During the eighteenth century, restrictions on Catholics were intensified by the enactment of Penal Laws, which were a charter in defense of Protestant power, and the main goal of these laws was to ensure that Catholics never again came to a position where they had power over Protestants. The provisions of these laws have strengthened the legal, political, economic and social inequality of Catholics and Protestants, and also deepened the gap between them, which is reflected in the conflicts in Northern Ireland. The Catholics were not allowed to vote, to manage schools, to obtain general or vocational education, to have occupations, to become teachers and to send their children to study abroad, to carry weapons, that is, swords that were an integral part of the attire of that time, to be members of the army, to possess a sporting rifle or pistol, or to have a horse worth more than £5; and if a Protestant admired a Catholic's horse on one occasion, he could simply take it, at that very price. With the introduction of these laws, there was a general opinion that Catholics would convert to Protestantism, which many did. Catholics were not allowed to own land, to buy or lease land, and in the event of such cases, the land was divided among all the children of the descendants in order to dismember it and prevent the emergence of great Catholic landowners. Only a handful of Catholics who owned the land survived, and Catholic peasants became residents of Protestant landowners. Marriages between Protestants and Catholics were declared null and void. Catholic bishops were persecuted, and Catholic churches were not allowed to have bell towers or fortifications. A new series of English Protestants had been installed, the new owners of land in Ireland became its ruling class. Economic and colonial subjugation of Ireland to Britain was complete with the division of the Irish population into Protestants (landowners and ruling class) and Catholics who were economically dependent and subordinate to them. In rural areas in the south, Protestants formed a secret sectarian society, the military peasant organization known as the "Whiteboys".

"In the 1870s it was estimated that a third of all the money in the Irish economy came from money sent by kindhearted Irish servant girls to their families. The Emigrant Industrial Savings Bank in New York alone would send more than $30 million to Ireland between 1850 and 1880.

Many families in Ireland owed their survival to what they gratefully called the "American Letter," a lifeline that helped them cope with brutal poverty and lack of opportunity." — Rashers Tierney

The history of Ireland acquired a much more complex and layered history in the recent, modern times. Of course, it was the natural trajectory of all the events that occurred throughout the preceding centuries. The Protestant Ascendancy of the 17th century was highly responsible in shaping the picture of the Ireland that emerged in the 18th and 19th centuries, laying the foundations for the crucial changes that were emerging. Let's go over the basics. Of course, we know that from 1801 to 1922, Ireland was a key part of the United Kingdom of Great Britain and Ireland. It was, for roughly the entirety of this period, controlled and governed by the United Kingdom Parliament in London, and through that parliament's administration in the Dublin Castle in Ireland. Sadly, the 19th century brought many hardships for the Irish people - as if they did not endure them in the centuries past. In many ways a modern, civilized era, the 19th century was one of the hardest tests for the people of Ireland, in a time when such a test should not have happened. The infamous Great Famine of the 1840's was just one of such difficulties, and one which we shall discuss later on. In this century, Ireland experienced a major decline in population, which endured for roughly a hundred years. Nevertheless, the Irish people, although fragmented and stricken with hardships, did not fail to hold on to their identity and to preserve their heritage in numerous ways. In the late 19th and early 20th century, difficulties continued, and Ireland was growing divided more and more. Irish Home Rule was established with legislation after numerous campaigns advocating for it, but it only saw a deepening of the existing conflict with Irish Unionists of Ulster, who were against it. Besides all this, Ireland was struck by mass waves of emigration, which were at a height during and following the Great Famine. The Irish-American diaspora was formed in these crucial years. And the difficulties only seemed to pile up. The early 1900's saw the outbreak of the First World War, the Great War to end all wars. The young men of Ireland were once more compelled to shed their blood and to continue the warrior's heritage of all their ancestors and the conflicts at home were put on hold for the duration of the war. Following those years of ghastly warfare, Ireland saw itself divided by increasingly militant Republican separatists. These tensions eventually erupted and culminated with a war in 1919, of which we shall talk more on the following pages. Nevertheless, from all this turmoil and struggle, the foundations of the modern Republic of Ireland were laid down in stone - the negotiations after the war led to the signing of the Anglo-Irish Treaty, resulting in five sixths of Ireland to secede from the United Kingdom, once more bringing independence to the Irish people after many centuries. Éirí Amach, the notorious Irish Rebellion of 1798, was the major event preceding the entrance into the 1800's and the new era of Irish history. It was one of the last major uprisings against English rule in Ireland. The Society of United Irishmen, a republican revolutionary group that was greatly influenced by the ideas of American and French Revolutions which swept over the world, was the main opponent of the English, rising up in arms against them. The French Revolutionary Wars were erupting across the world, ushering the future of Europe into a wholly new era, while the American Revolutionary wars of 1765-1783 were a major blow for the British Empire. Bolstered by these events, the Irish themselves wanted to taste the fresh water from the fountain of freedom. The Society of the United Irishmen was originally formed by radical Presbyterians that were angry for being shut out of power by the Anglicans and their establishment, and were subsequently joined by many oppressed and unhappy Irish of the Catholic population. The Rebellion of 1798 saw some swift initial success, especially in County Wexford near the coast, but was nevertheless suppressed by the militia of the government and the yeomanry forces, with major assistance from the British Army units. The rebellion, ending as a Government victory, was another major toll on Ireland's populace, resulting in up to 50,000 casualties. The rebellion was also another facet of the French-English conflict, as the French expeditionary force landed in County Mayo in support of the Rebels. However, the French too were defeated. Following the end of the rebellion, the Acts of the Union in 1800 was passed, which merged the Parliament of Ireland into the Parliament of the United Kingdom. Nevertheless, although it was swiftly and brutally suppressed, the Rebellion of 1798 was a major spark of hope for the oppressed and struggling Irish: it was followed by smaller uprisings such as the Irish Rebellion of 1803, and the Castle Hill Rebellion of 1804. Many agree that the events of 1798 were the foundation for increasing Irish plight for freedom.

However, Ireland had to enter into the 19th century still suffering the after effects of the 1798 rebellion. Irishmen, prisoners and indentured servants, were still being deported en-masse to Australia and the Carribean, and to America too.

"So does nobody care about Ireland?"
"Nobody. Neither King Louis, nor King Billie, nor King James." He nodded thoughtfully.
"The fate of Ireland will be decided by men, not a single one of whom gives a damn about her. That is her tragedy." — Edward Rutherfurd, The Rebels of Ireland

Robert Emmet's rebellion of 1803 was unsuccessful and caused further loss of life. The above mentioned Acts of the Union made Ireland a part of the British state - constitutionally, and can be seen as a major attempt to prevent further destabilisation of Britain. The Acts of the Union - passed by both the Irish Parliament and the Parliament of Great Britain, in 1800 - saw the abolishing of the Irish legislature and merging of the Kingdom of Ireland and the Kingdom of Great Britain into a single entity known as the United Kingdom of Great Britain and Ireland. The act passed in the Irish Parliament with a bit more difficulty and after a single failed attempt, but was nevertheless passed after much bribery. The same thing happened with the 1707 Acts of Union that united Scotland and England, where mass bribery was the crucial motivator. Bribery here was of course, peerage and titles, i.e. wealth. Following the union of the two Kingdoms, the majority of administration in Ireland was composed of people appointed to the positions by the central British government ensuring a firmer grip on the island. The major of these administration figures were the Lord Lieutenant of Ireland, representing the King, and the Chief Secretary of Ireland appointed by the British Prime Minister. The Civil Service in Ireland was also very important and was represented by the Under Secretary for Ireland. As time progressed, the British Parliament took over from the Monarch as the executive and legislative branch of the government. Due to this, the Chief Secretary in Ireland was a much more important figure than the Lord Lieutenant, whose role by then became much more symbolic. But what happened to the Irish Members of the Parliament after the Irish Parliament was abolished? They were subsequently elected to the House of Commons of the United Kingdom in Westminster, once more returning to serve their positions. The British Administration, known from the preceding centuries as "Dublin Castle", for their "headquarters", was mostly dominated by the Anglo-Irish establishment, until it was altogether removed from Dublin in 1922. Some of the old Penal Laws were still in use at the time in Ireland, and still discriminated against Irish Catholics. The Union's (with Great Britain) attraction for many of those discriminated Irish was the promise that the Penal Laws would be abolished, and that they would be granted a Catholic Emancipation, supposedly ending centuries of discrimination. However, this did not happen at the time, as it was blocked by King George III, who thought that granting the said Catholic Emancipation, he would break his oath - given at his coronation - that he would defend the Anglican Church in Ireland. This only resulted in continued conflict, as an Irish Catholic lawyer and politician, Daniel O'Connell, together with the Catholic Association led a campaign to abolish the Test Acts - the penal laws in use. A major breakthrough for the Irish Catholics was finally achieved with the help of Sir Arthur Wellesley, the famed First Duke of Wellington, and a notable Anglo-Irish statesman, and a soldier that gained immense fame for his victories against Napoleon. Wellesley used his influence, and immense political power as the then Prime Minister, to nudge the enabling of the needed legislation through the United Kingdom Parliament. Threatening resignation from his position, Wellesley persuaded King George IV to sign the document. This resulted in the Roman Catholic Relief Act of 1829, which finally allowed both British and Irish Catholics to sit in the Parliament and be represented. Daniel O'Connell thus became the first Irish Catholic MP to be seated in the Parliament for the first time since 1689. As the new head of the Repeal Association - a political movement fighting for the repeal of the Acts of Union - O'Connell began an unsuccessful campaign to repeal the acts and restore Irish self-government. These attempts at restoration by O'Connell were the true mirror of the times - they were peaceful, and relied on mass rallies, showcasing the majority supporting his campaign. No longer was war and conflict the answer as in centuries past. It was the efforts by O'Connell - although his campaign failed - that led to many important reforms within the government, most notable of these being the Poor Laws. However, violence cannot be avoided in history. Contrary to O'Connell's wishes, sporadic violence did break out across the nation, especially in the rural parts of the country. Ulster saw the brunt of these unrests, like the Dolly's Brae riot, a clash between the Orange Order and the Catholics.

Another aspect of this violence were the social unrests, which had a root in class differences. These social unrests saw the increasing rural populations coming into conflict with their landlords and the state, which eventually resulted in agrarian violence. Secret societies, composed mainly of the peasants, notably the previously mentioned Whiteboys, and the so-called Ribbonmen, relied on sabotage and violence in order to pressure their landlords into treating them better and providing more rights. One such outbreak of rural violence was known as the Tithe War, and appeared in the 1830's. It was a mostly peaceful campaign of civil disobedience, and resulted from the obligation of the mostly Catholic peasant class to pay tithes to the Protestant Church of Ireland. This resulted in the establishment of RIC - the Royal Irish Constabulary - that policed the rural areas and tried to keep the violence under control.

The 19th Century in Ireland

For much of the 19th century, Ireland experienced a big rollercoaster of ups and downs in economic terms. During the Napoleonic Wars it experienced an economic boom, which later crashed and resulted in a series of economic collapses and major famines that had a catastrophic toll on the civilian population. The last such major famine was in 1879, but the worst one was known as the Great Irish Famine, lasting from 1845 to 1851, and resulting in the deaths of roughly a million Irish, and the emigration of another million. It remains - to this very day - one of the hardest episodes in the history of Ireland. The roots of these economic issues lay in the fact that Ireland experienced a large population boom in the years prior, and the meager size of their properties and landholdings. This proved to be a fatal combination, especially if we take into account the social tradition of Ireland, the Gaelic heritage. It dictated that all sons of the family inherited equal parts of the family property. In time, this resulted in partition of landholdings into minute and insufficient crop lands. This was especially difficult with the aforementioned population boom. When the farms became so small, Irishmen could only choose to harvest a single crop. The most common choice was potato, as it could be used to feed a family and grown in ample amounts even on the small plot of land.

"The dependence of the Irish upon the potato was clearly a dangerous trend. Just how dangerous was to be proven in the years 1845 to 1850, when intermittent blight struck the country and destroyed what was for

many their sole food supply. The ensuing famine and misery is beyond description. By 1855, the population has dropped by two million, lost to starvation, disease, and emigration. Between 1850 and 1890, a further two million individuals emigrated to North America, Australia and Britain, and few of them ever returned." - Oonagh Walsh

This issue was even deepened through the rise of land enclosures, and also through overgrazing of cattle, which resulted in even smaller size of plots and arable land available to tenants. With all these issues combined the stage was set for the devastating effects following the outbreak of the famine. And when it occurred, many Irish sought to flee their native island in search of a better future overseas. America saw a large influx of Irish people, who became one of the most notable minorities in the United States, besides the Italians. Another fact that contributed to such major loss of life during the famine, known also as the potato blight, was the poor response from the government. During the time, in the new "Whig" government, the assistant secretary to the Treasury, one Charles Trevelyan, was the man largely responsible for the British Government's response to the famine. When the latter swept across the island, rural populace was left entirely without food, facing certain death. Sadly, the then Prime Minister, Lord John Russell, clung to a strict economic policy. He believed that further intervention of the state would take a big toll on the economy, as the nation would be entirely dependent on handouts. And even though Ireland in the years preceding had a major net surplus of food produced, most of it was exported - to England and elsewhere in Europe. The whole situation took on a hellish and catastrophic turn when bouts of cholera, dysentery, and typhoid fever broke out across the nation and took hold. Donations poured in from across the world, and from some highly important individuals, but it didn't prove to be enough or at the right time - the Irish nation and its people were suffering a devastating fate. And the root of that fate lay in the inadequate approach by the British Government. And it wasn't only death that took a toll on Ireland's populace - it was emigration too. In the years before the famine, emigration was somewhat common, but not in large numbers. Men went to seek labor overseas, especially into North America, Canada, and Great Britain. But with the Great Famine sweeping across the land, emigration took a new and unparalleled scale. Australia too became a popular location to emigrate to. Nevertheless, America saw the greatest influx of Irish immigrants. Many established themselves in New York and Chicago, and elsewhere. In New York, Irish were a major faction and noted in the Five Points burrough, where Irish street gangs competed for domination with the native ones. Sadly, many of Ireland's sons emigrated to America only to be embroiled in a new conflict. Escaping a difficult life in Ireland, they were enlisted to fight in the American Civil War as soon as they would arrive on American soil. In time, a major Irish diaspora formed in the United States, and led to those influential members of it to directly fund the Irish independence movement back home. Around 1858, the IRB - Irish Republican Brotherhood - known also as the Fenians, was formed and devoted to rebel against the British. This conflict was not only reserved to the United Kingdom - it spread into the diaspora as well. New York's Irish organisation - the Clan na Gael - raided into the British Province of Canada. Further unrests followed, with some appearing during the height of the famine in Ireland. The movement known as Young Irelanders, composed of members of the Repeal Association, formed a new "Irish Confederation", and made attempts to launch a full scale rebellion against the British, in 1848. With the famine situation ongoing, the British resorted to military intervention. The revolt only deepened the crisis. The rebellion's leader, William Smith O'Brien, was soon after arrested alongside his companions, and was sentenced to transportation to Van Diemen's Land, today known as Tasmania, off the coast of Australia. Many Irishmen found their way to these distant lands. Even after the worst of the famine was done, many Irish chose to leave the island altogether, searching for a better fate. Those that stayed continued to struggle, and many died. A struggle was almost constant, and the Irish farmers fought a bitter campaign to ensure better rights and land redistribution by the government. This campaign was called the "Land War", and had deep underlying social and economic aspects. A solution was sorely needed in Ireland - the majority of the land owners in Ireland were originally Protestant settlers from England, a fact which created a deep social divide. During this time, history came back to haunt the inhabitants of Ireland: the poor and struggling farmers recalled the past, believing that the farmland had been unjustly taken from their ancestors, during the English conquests of the island. Around this time, the Irish National Land League emerged, a movement created to defend and fight for the interests of poor tenant farmers. What they demanded from the government were the so-called "three Fs": Fair rent, Free sale, and Fixity of tenure. The movement involved some members from groups such as the Irish Republican Brotherhood, and other prominent national leaders such as Charles Stewart Parnell. The struggle for better tenant rights quickly got a national character, and many saw the potential for popular mobilisation.

Did You Know?

"During the Great Irish Famine, donations for the struggling folk of Ireland came from all over the world. Over £2,000,000 were collected! Did you know that during this time, a special bond between the Irish and the Choctaw people was created? The Choctaw, a Native American tribe, although suffering greatly in their own homeland, still managed to collect a sum of roughly $170 – which equals to around $5,000 today. Their humbleness and selfless generosity inspired the Irish people and created a lasting friendship between the two nations. In 2018, Ireland created a scholarship for Choctaw youth, sending a message to all Choctaw that "their kindness has never been and never will be – forgotten in Ireland."

A lavish monument commemorating this friendship, titled "Kindred Spirits", has been erected in Castleredmond, Midleton, in County Cork."

One of the most notable tactics that the Land League utilized in their struggle for rights, was the so-called boycott, a term which originates from Ireland and from this very period. Boycott meant that unpopular landlords were ostracized from the community by the locals, and thus pressured. Nevertheless, some Land League members still resorted to violence in their struggle and attempted to forcefully push their struggle. When landlords attempted to evict the tenants in response, the situation would often escalate into armed confrontation. In order to contain this violence the British Government, under the leadership of Prime Minister Benjamin Disraeli, introduced the so-called Irish Coercion Act, which acted as a form of martial law. Many of the prominent Irish national leaders such as Davitt, Parnell, and William O'Brien, were imprisoned under suspicions of leading the violence and unrest. Nevertheless, the land question was ultimately settled through the Irish Land Acts. First of these was the Landlord and Tenant (Ireland) Act, brought in 1870, and followed with the Land Law (Ireland) in 1881 brought by William Ewart Gladstone. The latter was the first act to introduce extensive new rights to tenant farmers, which was one of the major breakthroughs for the Irish people. The Wyndham Land Purchase Act of 1903 that was won by William O'Brien after the 1902 Land Conference was another major breakthrough, and allowed tenant farmers to purchase their plots of land from their landlords. The Bryce Labourers (Ireland) Act from 1906 followed and largely resolved the problems of non-existent rural housing. Through all these acts, the Irish countryside was now filled with a large class of small property owners. This in turn, dissipated the power of the old Anglo-Irish landed gentry class after so many decades of Irish struggle for equal rights. In 1908, a new act was delivered, the J.J. Clancy Town Housing Act, which boosted the building of urban council housing, further improving the situation of the Irish. Thus it was, that in time, and through a devoted struggle for their own freedom, the Irish managed to achieve a string of acts that worked to their benefit. Agricultural advancements were also made, initiated by Horace Plunkett, and evolved after the passing of the Local Government (Ireland) Act in 1898, an act that placed the running of rural affairs into local hands. Still, all these acts did not extinguish the Irish passionate desire for independence as the British had hoped. Because, for the Irish people, freedom and independence were the most coveted desires they kept - and they were determined to get them.

"I calculate that one third of the people of Dublin are underfed; that half the children attending Irish primary schools are ill-nourished.... I suppose there are twenty thousand families in Dublin in whose domestic economy milk and butter are all but unknown: black tea and dry bread are their staple articles of diet. There are many thousand fireless hearth places in Dublin on the bitterest days of winter; there would be many thousand more only for such bodies as the Society of St. Vincent de Paul. Twenty thousand Dublin families live in one room tenements. It is common to find two or three families occupying the same room; and sometimes one of the families will have a lodger! There are tenement rooms in Dublin in which over a dozen persons live, eat, and sleep... The tenement houses of Dublin are so rotten that they periodically collapse upon their inhabitants, and if the inhabitants collect in the streets to discuss matters, the police baton them to death." – Patrick Pearse

During the 19th century, the Irish culture in general was undergoing a massive and cardinal change. As the famine affected primarily the poorest classes in rural Ireland such as those that still used the Gaelic Irish language as their mother tongue, and caused heavy loss of life amongst these persons. This led in turn to a major decline in use of Irish. The language was further suppressed from the 1830's and on, when National Schools arose across the country. However, the classes in these schools were in English, and use of Irish was strictly forbidden. Thus, even though literacy was encouraged in society, it was done in English. A further toll on the language was taken through emigration, as large numbers of people left Ireland for good, especially from the

Gaeltacht regions in the south. Once these Irish were settled in overseas countries, like America, they gradually stopped using Gaelic, after a few generations. With all these aspects combined, the Gaelic language was no longer the majority tongue in Ireland by 1900 - for the first time in roughly 2,000 years. Its decline was steady in the following decades. By the time Ireland finally gained its independence, Gaelic language was isolated and used only in the Gaeltacht regions on the western seaboard of Ireland. In an attempt to save the Irish language from extinction - it being the major part of Irish identity - the Irish nationalists began a comprehensive program of Gaelic revival in the late 19th century. Today, the Irish language is experiencing a steady ascent to the status it once had. Did you know that on the popular language-learning platform, Duolingo, the Irish language learning course has more people learning Irish than there are native Irish? This is one clear proof of the language's rising popularity and unique character.

"The Organisation and the Government are pledged to coordinate,democratize and Gaelicize our education. In each of these aims great progress has already been made. It is now possible for the child of the poorest parents to pass from one end of the educational ladder to the other, and the Irish language has been restored to its own place in Irish education. In addition, the condition of that important class, the Secondary Teachers, has been improved. The Organisation and Government intend to devote special attention to the problem of safeguarding the Language in the Gaeltacht by improving economic conditions in the Gaeltacht and developing Educational Institutions therein."

The Birth of the Republic: Politics and Conflict in 20th Century Ireland

In the late 19th and early 20th century, politics were at an all time high where internal affairs are considered. Up until the 1870's, those Irish who were elected as MP's (Members of Parliament) were either Conservatives or Liberals, and belonged to the main British political parties. In 1859, the Conservatives won the majority vote in the Irish general elections. A significant minority vote also went to the so-called Unionists who strongly adhered to the Acts of the Union and resisted any and all attempts to dilute it in any way. In the 1870's, a new movement was formed by a nationalist campaigner called Isaac Butt. This new moderate nationalist movement was known as the Home Rule league. When Butt died, leading Irish political figures, Charles Steward Parnell, and William Shaw, turned that home rule movement, which was then known as the Irish Parliamentary Party (IPP), into a major political force and a major player in Irish internal affairs. This party subsequently came to dominate Irish politics. Its growing strength and influence amongst the people was first shown in the 1880 general elections, when the party won 63 seats in the Parliament. By 1885 this increased to 86 seats in the parliament. This movement headed by Parnell proved to be a broad one, including those from the Land League as well as conservative landowners. Parnell was also involved in campaigning for the right for Ireland to govern itself as a region within the United Kingdom, a policy that came in direct conflict with those who wanted to completely repeal the Act of Union. In the end it was this Home Rule policy that essentially divided Ireland. This created a complex political picture in Ireland, with Unionists based in Ulster opposing it, and the Orange Order mobilizing the opposition. These tensions escalated in 1886, when major riots broke out in Belfast. Parnell was later involved in a major public scandal, one which split the IPP in half. The political system was then divided into those who supported Parnell, and those who were against him. In essence, the country grew separated politically, largely dominated by those for the Home Rule policy, and the Ulster Unionists' opposition to it. By 1914, this tense situation escalated into militancy, with both sides openly arming themselves and conducting drills and exercises in preparation of a conflict. This brought on the period known as the Home Rule Crisis. Even though Irish politics was heavily dominated by nationalism, the social and economic issues in Ireland were far from over. Dublin, for example, was a city known for both its severe poverty and its severe wealth - a true city of paradox. Dublin became the home of some of the United Kingdom's worst slums and most decadent quarters. It boasted the largest red light district in the world, known as the Monto, or Montgomery Street. Unemployment was rampant, and Ireland was in a bad state in the early 20th century.

The world was entering a deadly and vicious war in the early 20th century. The "war to end all wars", the Great War, would sweep over the world and leave no nation untouched. At the time, Ireland was in an almost chaotic state, and on the brink of civil war - heavily divided over the Home Rule policy. Nationalists and Unionists were ready to clash at any moment. 100,000 unionists, led by barrister Sir Edward Carson, formed the Ulster Volunteers in April 1912 to oppose Home Rule. Carson and James Craig organized the "Ulster Covenant" in September, with over 470,000 people signing a pledge to oppose Home Rule. In January 1913, this movement founded the Ulster Volunteer Force (UVF). 30,000 German rifles with 3,000,000 cartridges arrived at Larne in April 1914, with the authorities being blockaded by the UVF. The Curragh Incident demonstrated that using the British army to force Ulster into home rule from Dublin would be impossible. As a result, Irish nationalists formed the Irish Volunteers, a forerunner of the Irish Republican Army. When the Great War was in its opening stages, in September 1914, the United Kingdom Parliament at last passed on the Government of Ireland Act of 1914, which was meant to establish self-government for Ireland. The dissident nationalists condemned it as a "partition deal". However, as the war raged on, the Act was suspended for its duration - as the British expected that the war would last for only a year. They were wrong however, as the war raged on for several and took an immense toll in casualties for the United Kingdom as a whole. The Great War now placed opposing Irish parties fighting side by side on the fronts of Western Europe. The Irish Regiments were a part of the British Army, which saw service all across the global theaters of war. The Irishmen would serve with valour in many of the major battles of the war. Most notable Irish units were the 16th and 10th Irish Divisions, and the 36th Ulster Division. They all suffered immense casualties on the Western Front trenches, and especially at Gallipoli. It is believed that roughly 35,000 to 50,000 Irishmen died in the Great War in service against the enemy. Their sacrifice will never be forgotten.

Thousands of Irish nationalists fought bravely for Britain in World War I, but no unit suffered as badly as the Ulster unit at the Battle of the Somme in 1916. But it is also true that most of the Irish did not participate in the war against Germany. Nevertheless, this was also not an expression of the position of convinced Republicans, for whom the difficulties of England were always a chance for Ireland. The words of Padrake Pierce perfectly summed this up: *"to achieve independence the Irish will need a "bloody sacrifice".* The condition was complicated in the run-up to the Easter Rising. The rebellion was called off by the chief of the "Irish Volunteers," and efforts to recruit German forces were unsuccessful. The German weapons ship Aud was captured, and Sir

Roger Casement, who was attempting to put down the insurrection because he thought it was premature, was apprehended by the British after disembarking from a German submarine. Before battling for Irish independence, Casement was a powerful British colonial officer. As a spy, he was executed. The infamous "Black Diaries" tainted his image (still classified as secret). In the face of the fact that the rebellion was destined to fail, the Irish Republican Brotherhood (IRB) vowed not to call it off. This complicated situation was akin to a boiling pot ready to explode at any given moment. The tension finally erupted in the Easter Week, in April 1916, and turned into the famed *Easter Rising* of 1916, known also as the Easter Rebellion. In Irish it is known as *Éirí Amach na Cásca.* The rebellion was launched by Irish Republicans, seeking to finally establish an independent Irish Republic free of British Rule. It was one of the most significant armed uprisings in Ireland since the 1798 rebellion, and the first conflict in a turbulent period in Irish history known as the Irish Revolutionary Period. The uprising generally failed, and sixteen of its leaders were executed one month later, in May of 1916. However, the Easter Rising had a major echo that could not be stopped, and its effects were mirrored in the increasing popularity of the idea of Irish independence.

Although the Easter Uprising of 1916 attracted public sympathy, it did not bring immediate changes in the political situation. The Irish nationalists of Redmond were still seen as political spokesmen, and Home Rule was seen as the aspirations of the Catholic Irish. The situation began to change in 1917. An important factor was the appearance on the political arena of Michael Collins (Mícheál Ó Coileáin), an extremely capable organizer of the Irish Republican Brotherhood, and a man who saw the futility of armed uprisings, since they had little chance of success. Collins was a militant Republican, but he was supported by non-violent Sinn Fein members such as Arthur Griffith, who were not involved in the events of 1916. These people believed that Home Rule was not enough to fulfill the Irish hopes, and the British should cede their rights to a republic of 32 counties. So they decided to challenge Redmond's party in a by-election. The first, in County Roscommon, culminated in a convincing Republican victory, soon followed by another in County Longford. Such victories inevitably influenced the gradual change in the sympathies of the Irish population - from Redmond to nationalists. The British unknowingly helped this process by freeing all surviving prisoners who took part in the Easter Rising in July 1917 (they were in prison in England). Unlike 1916, on their return to Dublin they were greeted as heroes. Among them were the main figures in the struggle for Irish independence. Their convictions had nothing to do with constitutional nationalism, so it was difficult to hope for a compromise.

Did You Know?

"Patrick Henry Pearse (Pádraig Anraí Mac Piarais; 10 November 1879 – 3 May 1916), was one of the foremost leaders of the Eastern Rising of 1916. A man of many passions, he was a teacher, a barrister, a writer and a poet, as well as a political activist. Patrick Pearse was the man instrumental in many developments during the short-lived Easter Rebellion, and was the one to read the "Proclamation of the Irish Republic" at the headquarters of the rising. He was chosen as the President of that Republic as well. Alas, he was also the one to proclaim surrender after just six days of heavy fighting. Pearse, alongside fourteen other leaders of the uprising, were executed by firing squad. Ever since, his memory lives on with the Irish, and he is seen as the embodiment of that iconic Irish spirit of freedom and fight for independence."

The events of the Easter Rising and the subsequent revolutionary period culminated in the Irish Civil War. Known as the *Cogadh Cathartha na hÉireann,* this civil war lasted from 1922 to 1923, and was waged between the Irish Republican Army (IRA), and the Provisional Government. The conflict once more separated Ireland and its people, and pitted them against one another. It left big marks on Irish society and divided it for generations to follow. *Today,* two of the main political parties in the Republic of Ireland, Fine Gael and Fianna Fáil, are direct descendants of the opposing sides of the war.

The Irish Free State arose from the civil war of 1922-1923, and the resentment of the opposition tainted the new country's early years. This resentment stemmed partially from the defeats suffered by both sides during the civil war, but it also stemmed from de Valera and his supporters' refusal to establish a new political system. The Irish Free State (1922 to 1937) emerged in a time when Europe was filled with dictatorships, and the world was on the brink of a new deadly conflict. It also experienced a major economic downturn during this period. Nevertheless, Ireland – i.e. the Irish Free State – remained a democracy during this time. This democracy was clearly shown in the 1932 general elections, when *Fianna Fáil*, the losing faction of the civil war, led by *Éamon de Valera,* won the vote and took power peacefully. This final, peaceful change of government in 1932 was the final cue for the people of Ireland to accept the creation of the Free State and the partition – Northern Ireland was to remain in the United Kingdom.

By 1937, a new Constitution re-established the Irish Free State as Ireland, known in Irish as *Éire.* After centuries of hardships, Ireland was finally emerging from its struggles and settling onto the path of an independent and free nation. Nevertheless, the Second World War broke out and placed Europe into the deadly jaws of global war. Ireland managed to avoid the brunt of this ravaging conflict by remaining neutral. This protected the still new nation from an uncertain fate during the war, but nevertheless, tens of thousands of Irish volunteered to serve overseas, with the British forces. Of course, Ireland too felt the effects of the world economic struggles during the war – food rationing and coal shortages were commonplace.

In 1949, Ireland officially left the Commonwealth of Nations association and was formally declared the Republic of Ireland. Ever since, it has been on a steady rise as a free, independent, and flourishing

Irish nation – finally breathing free after centuries of a desperate struggle for freedom.

The History of the Irish in America

When a people endures so many struggles and turmoil – like the Irish did – solutions and exits become few and far in between. Over the centuries, many Irish sought solutions by leaving their native island behind along with all its turmoils. Some emigrated freely, others were exiled to penal colonies while some were sent overseas as indentured servants. Their fates were uncertain, and the new lands were so different from old Ireland. Nevertheless, a new chapter in the history of Ireland was begun. Some ended in Australia, others in Britain, the Carribean, in Chile, Mexico, and mostly – in North America. In time, a substantial Irish diaspora emerged, centered in the United States, that created a whole new facet of the Irish history and identity, and one which cannot be overlooked today. In 2019, around 32 million Americans identified as Irish. This makes for roughly 9.7% of the entire population – a number that certainly tells us of the number of Irish that emigrated to this then distant land.

In the slowly emerging American cities of the late 1700's and early 1800's, the Irish immigrants were the first substantial ethnic minority to arrive. However, their arrival was not one of grandeur and splendor. Many of the emigrating Irish believed that the situation overseas could not be as bad as it was in Ireland – but the truth was somewhat different. Once in America, the Irish had to start from the very bottom – struggling their way up in the social hierarchy. Men were usually employed in manual labor, while women worked as maids. Sadly, the newly arrived Irish often lived in difficult conditions in America, especially in the metropolis cities such as Chicago and New York. Seeking a better fate in this new land, they were instead tossed into a whole new mess, with difficulties just increasing. The Irish almost exclusively lived in crowded conditions, in the poorest quality housing estates in circumstances that readily communicated disease, violence, alcoholism, and crime. The already harsh conditions of these towns in America did not give the Irish a chance at a better, honest or pure life. Instead, America's conditions molded them accordingly, fitting them into an already existing network of crime and poverty. But the Irish were always ready to adapt and to overcome any conditions. Still, many of the natives of these cities did not like the newly arriving Irish – they would often move out of Irish neighborhoods altogether, and were quick to stereotype them as alcoholics, brawlers, and ruffians without making an effort to understand the Irish soul or their difficult position. In those early years of Irish settlement in America, plenty of discrimination appeared against the Irish, making their lives all the more difficult. Employment barriers began appearing. It wasn't all that rare to see a shop looking for workers, but with a sign that said "No Irish Need Apply". The jobs that the Irish did manage to find were menial, hard, dirty, and underpaid – simply put, these were the jobs that no one else were willing to do. It can be a big understatement to say that the lives of the Irish immigrants in America were tough. A popular quote of the times said that you "seldom see a grey haired Irishman". That is because their average lifespan in those early days was roughly 40 years on average. Getting out of that rut was a long and trying process – but the Irish persevered. Each new generation gave efforts to establish themselves, to place the Irish firmly and proudly into American society, standing shoulder to shoulder with all the other ethnicities of that vast nation. In time, the Irish managed to achieve success in politics of the United States as well, where some Irishmen managed to reach influential positions of power by the middle of the 19th century, just a generation or two after the main influx of Irish settlers. In just a few decades that followed, Irish were a dominant part of the political "machines" in the big cities of America – such as Boston, Chicago, New York, and similar metropolitan areas. Sadly, most other Irish Americans – those not involved in politics – were still living a life of poverty and hardship, still resorting to those menial jobs of hard labor and domestic service. One of the most famous Irish American families that managed to rise in this period are the Kennedys. The first of that family arrived from Ireland in 1848 – as mere laborers. They lived in struggle and died in struggle. However, the following generations worked hard, and managed to reach positions of power with slow and measured steps. The grandson of that first Kennedy to have arrived, managed to reach college and make a name for himself – he was Joseph P. Kennedy, a prominent US politician, investor, and businessman, whose descendants, like John F. Kennedy, were instrumental in the politics of the United States, and the world. Alas, such prominence was not enjoyed by all Irish – and those that rose in power were just a minor fraction of the total population of Irish-Americans.

Did You Know?

"The modern Goose Island in Chicago in the USA was originally the core of Irish immigrants in that city. Originally known as Kilgubbin, after the Kilgobbin Cross in Ireland's Dublin Region, (Cill Ghobáin), the island became the center of Irish in Chicago, from where they spread to the other parts of the city. At the end of the 19th century, Kilgubbin was known as "Little Hell", and was a safe haven for shady characters and criminals, becoming one of the largest shanty towns of the region. It was known for the numerous geese that were kept there, alongside other animals. Did you know that the infamous Irish-American mobster, Dean O'Banion, was raised on Kilgubbin, where his lengthy career began. Dean O'Banion was a notorious figure and the main rival of mobsters Johnny Torrio and Al Capone."

The largest numbers of Irish emigrated into America during the period between 1820 and 1860, when Ireland was struck by numerous economic hardships. Poverty in Ireland – in Dublin especially – was so dismal at the time that it bordered inhuman conditions. Some of the reports from that time paint a shocking image of poverty in Ireland, where one has to wonder just how did the people carry on in such conditions. One reporter, visiting a poor family near the town of Midleton in County Cork, wrote of his experience:

"I went into several hovels... They all consisted of mud walls, with a covering of rafters and straw. None of them so good as the place where you keep your little horse. I took a particular account of the first place that I went into. It was twenty-one feet long and nine feet wide. The floor, the bare ground. No fireplace, no chimney, the fire (made of potato haulm [i.e. potato stems]) made on one side against the wall, and the smoke going out of the hole in the roof. No table, no chair; I sat to write upon a block of wood. Some stones for seats. No goods but a pot and a shallow tub, for the pig and the family both to eat out of. There was one window, nine inches by five, and the glass half broken out."

Understanding such depravity of life back in Ireland, one cannot at all be surprised about the massive emigration that took place in the 19th century. From 1820 to 1860, roughly 2,000,000 Irish arrived in America, fleeing horrible living conditions. A total of 75% of those 2,000,000 – that's one and a half million people – arrived in America after the Great Irish Famine struck Ireland between 1845 and 1852. Many of these were sons of poor farmers and illiterate people who had little chance of succeeding in Ireland. Looking for a better life, they would gather as much money as was possible (often little or none) and set upon the transatlantic ships bound for America. Sadly, these were no luxury ocean voyages. Many Irish died en route from Ireland to the United States, without ever setting foot on that new continent. They perished on the ships, due to the horrible conditions on board, with disease and hunger rampant. These ships became known as *coffin ships.* Those that did arrive – in their millions – were quick to choose the largest American cities to settle in. That way, they would ensure an establishment of their own, tight knit, Irish communities, which would allow them to support each other and protect their own interests and people. The cities that had the largest number of Irish settlers were New York, Boston, and Philadelphia, followed by Detroit, Chicago, Baltimore, Pittsburgh, St. Paul, St. Louis, San Francisco, and others. Still, many chose not to settle, and moved westwards with the expansion into the vast territories of the North American continent. Arguably, those that chose to go westwards, enjoyed a better – although still hard – life than those that lived in the squalid conditions of the big cities. Those Irish that wanted to work, could easily find employment with the westward expansion. By 1854, the US government opened up the Kansas Territory to new settlers, which attracted a large number of Irish immigrants. They moved with the expansion of railroads, on which they usually worked as hard laborers. The westward expansion required strong and physically able men in order to carry out the massive construction works and building of railroads – and Irish were quick to apply. Cities sprang up, and these Irishmen often settled in them for good. Kansas City is one such town that was built by the Irish immigrants. Today, a good deal of its populace can trace its descent to the Irish.

Sadly, the United States themselves were about to experience a rough chapter in their history. Those Irish that arrived were to experience it the same as every other ethnicity of America – firsthand. The American Civil War, lasting from 1861 to 1865, saw plenty of Irishmen fighting on the battlefields. Some were second, or even third generation Irish, while others were fresh immigrants, born in Ireland and fighting in a war they knew nothing about. In the Union Army there were at least 38 Union regiments that had "Irish" in their name. In that same army, there were roughly 145,000 soldiers who were born in Ireland. Anecdotes tell that the young Irishmen that stepped off the boats in cities such as New York and Chicago were at once recruited into the army and sent into action, just moments after docking. Many would die soon after – it was a sad fate for many.

"Well it's by the hush, me boys, and be sure to hold your noise
And listen to poor Paddy's sad narration
I was by hunger pressed and in poverty distressed
So I took a thought I'd leave the Irish nation
Well I sold me horse and cow, my little pigs and sow
My father's plot of land I then departed
And me sweetheart Bid McGee I'm afraid I'll never see
For I left her there that morning broken hearted
Here ye boys, now take my advice
To Americay I'll have ye not be going
There is nothing here but war where the murderin' cannons roar
And I wish I was at home in dear old Dublin..."

In modern times, with the rise of the Irish in America and their acceptance into society, have undergone a subtle cultural and biological assimilation over the generations. Today, it has become difficult to determine precisely who is Irish, and the 100% pure Irish genealogy amongst Irish-Americans is rare and almost non-existent. A good insight for this is the fact that in the 1860's only one tenth of Irishmen chose to marry outside of their own ethnicity. In the 1960's, however, a century later, a half of all Irish-American men were married to women of different ethnic backgrounds. Those descended from the original Irish settlers include those who are today classified under altogether different ethnic groups. Interestingly there is an immense part of the modern American populace that simply cannot identify its ethnicity whatsoever at the census survey. Much of the data that is available on Irish-Americans today is based on those people who simply chose to identify as Irish on the census bureau surveys. These people may or may not be typical of the original descendants of Ireland. Still, those who can trace their origins to Irish immigrants with accuracy are getting rarer in America today, and their Irish genetics are usually no longer that – with generations of intermarrying with diverse ethnicities, the descendants of the original Irish immigrants are now distinctly *American*.

Nevertheless, it is clear that the Irish and their descendants in America became a crucial part in the overall history of Ireland, and – so to speak – its distinct branch outside of the bounds of the island of Ireland. It became clear that, after emerging from the first few decades of squalor and poverty in America, the Irish-Americans came to a rise in its society, eventually surpassing the American standards of income and education. For example, Irish-American incomes have been roughly 5% above the national average in the 1970's. Furthermore, the number of schooling years, and the number of Irish-Americans in college are roughly the same as the US population as a whole. What's more, the IQ scores of the Irish-Americans are consistently just above the national norm of 100 – and have been so for the past 50 years. Alas, one negative aspect remains widespread amongst Irish-Americans and Irish in general – and that is *alcoholism*. In America, it is a prevalent and striking characteristic amongst Irish-Americans. Contemporary studies have shown that the rates of alcohol consumption and alcohol related diseases are much higher amongst Irish-American than they are in other ehtnic groups in the United States, such as the Germans, Italians, or Jews. Nevertheless, they remain an exemplary ethnic group in this country, and one of the ethnicities that were – by and large – responsible for the creation of the modern United States of America as we know it today. Today, their heritage is alive and well, and experiencing a steady boom with each new generation of Irish-Americans.

One of the most appropriate ways to end this segment on Irish-Americans and their history is with a poem. *"Spancil Hill"* is a traditional Irish folk song composed by Michael Considine (1850 to 1873), and Irishman who immigrated to America. His story is a tragic one, and is a perfect – although tragic – insight into the fate of the millions of Irishmen who set sail for the distant American shores. Spancil Hill of the song is located in Muckinish townland, in the parish of Clooney in County Clare in Ireland. Michael Considine was born there in 1850, at the end of the Great Irish Famine, into a family of tenant farmers who lived close to the Spancil Hill fair grounds. Like many of his compatriots, Considine chose to emigrate to America, leaving Ireland in 1870, when he was 20 years old. His intention was to earn as much money in America as he could, so he could afford to return to Ireland and marry his sweetheart, who was left home waiting for him. Michael Considine arrived in Boston and worked there for two years before moving on to California, where his health began to suffer due to the harsh living conditions and hard labor. Realizing that he was going to die in America, never again to return to Ireland and see his sweetheart, Michael Considine penned a touching poem which became a symbol of the Irish plight in America. Not long after sending a letter to his relatives in Ireland – with the poem included – young Michael died in California, aged just twenty-three. His tragic fate was shared by many young Irishmen who immigrated to America. This poem serves to remind us of their tragic fate, preserving the memory for generations to come. Below is the version of the poem as immortalized by the legendary Irish music group, *The Dubliners.*

"Last night as I lay dreaming of pleasant days gone by
Me mind being bent on rambling, to Ireland I did fly
I stepped on board a vision, and I followed with a will
'Til next I came to anchor at the cross at Spancil Hill
It being on the 23rd of June, the day before the fair
When Ireland's sons and daughters and friends assembled there
The young, the old, the brave and the bold came, their duty to fulfill
At the parish church in Clooney, a mile from Spancil Hill
I went to see me neighbors, to see what they might say
The old ones were all dead and gone, the young ones turning gray
But I met the tailor Quigley, he's as bold as ever still

Ah, he used to mend me britches when I lived in Spancil Hill
I paid a flying visit to my first and only love
She's as white as any lily, gentle as a dove
And she threw her arms around me saying, "Johnny, I love you still"
Ah she's Nell the farmer's daughter and the pride of Spancil Hill
I dreamed I held and kissed her as in the days of yore
'Ah Johnny, you're only jokin', as many's the time before
Then the cock, he crew in the morning, he crew both loud and shrill
And I awoke in California, many miles from Spancil Hill..."

The Enigmatic Mythology and Folklore of Ireland

As we all know, history and mythology are indivisible – they go hand in hand through centuries, together carving out an identity of a nation. Many times the myths of a nation have roots in actual historical events, serving as a memory and a reminder of that people's most distant origins. For the Irish people, their rich folklore, legends, and mythology, were all very important in the preservation of their identity throughout the centuries of struggle they endured. Also, they are a clear cross-cut section that allows us a clear view into the many different historical periods and the diverse peoples that now make up the bulk of the Irish genetics. The well preserved Irish mythology has diverse elements, many of which hail from the oldest inhabitants of the island and their own beliefs. With the arrival of the Celtic culture to the island, this mythology gains an even deeper, richer dimension and emerges as a world full of complex stories, legendary heroes, and tales of daring and magic. In certain parts of the mythology, we can read of successive waves of peoples that arrived to Ireland – a part that certainly has roots in actual history. However, through time and legend, these peoples have attained magical properties and have been demonized and made larger-than-life. It is also important to note that much of this mythology has roots in pre-Christian Ireland, but has survived in large part thanks to the advent of Christianity. This fact is somewhat paradoxical but is true – the introduction of Christianity to the island helped with the appearance of writing and literacy, and this gave a chance for the myths to be written down for posterity. This was often done by monks themselves. Many of Ireland's iconic legends were penned down in early Irish manuscripts, and form the bulk of Irish medieval literature.

However, much of the traditional folklore, and the mythology, has been preserved by oral tradition, down through the generations. Faced with hardships and numerous invaders, the Irish people clung dearly to the most precious parts of their identity. This oral tradition is known as *Béaloideas*. All in all, the Irish mythology has been so well preserved that it can be researched and experienced in detail. Four cycles have been identified, which are all distinct and sometimes overlapping. Of these we shall talk in detail. Besides the four cycles, there are plenty of texts, tales, and legends that don't belong in any of them, and are still important on their own. Today, the Irish myths and legends have become one of the most iconic, recognizable, and important aspects of the Irish identity and history. Since this is a book on Celtic history and the History of Ireland, we cannot overlook this highly valuable source of information on the Irish people and their rich and dramatic history.

In the following lines, we shall do our very best to cover some of the most important features of the rich Irish mythology, and to mention some of the iconic creatures from the Irish folklore, which serve as a veritable mirror of the Irish people and the centuries of their formation. Of course, these are not all the myths and all the creatures – listing them all would take a lot, lot, more space and time. Today, some of the best known tales and myths are those of the heroic *Fionn MacCumhaill,* the mythical hunter and warrior; the daring *Táin Bó Cúailnge* – known as the Cattle Raid of Cooley; the *Tír na nÓg,* a Celtic underworld; the *Tuatha Dé Danann Gods; Na Fianna; Aes Sídhe;* the story of the hero *Cú Chulainn,* and many, many others.

Before the arrival of Christianity, the bulk of the Irish folklore was mainly composed from the many stories and legends that were passed down orally by the Druids – the important characters in Celtic social structure - until the 7th century, when monks started gathering and writing them down. This was a process that lasted decades. Since written records appear in Ireland at a very early age, many of these myths and legends, and beliefs, have been preserved in stunning detail, allowing us to research them with accuracy and to draw many important parallels with the Indo-European myths in general. As mentioned, these tales and myths are divided into four chronological periods – or *cycles*. There are several distinctions within each main cycle, and there are many mythological texts that do not belong to either cycle. Furthermore, there are several folk tales that, while not entirely mythological, contain characters from one or more periods, and that makes them an equally important part of the mythology.

The earliest accounts about the invasion and settlement of Ireland by many diverse tribes (considered as a race of demigods) from ancient times to the arrival of the Celts are included in the **Mythological Cycle.** The next one is the **Ulster Cycle** - these are the tales of Ireland's early days, and they are famous and entertaining in character. These are probably the most popular of all Irish tales, containing the adventures of Cuchulainn and other famed heroes, as well as the story of *Táin* (Cattle Raid of Cooley). Within the **Fenian Cycle,** the soldiers of *Fianna*, led by *Fionn MacCumhaill,* wander Ireland and execute miraculous and valiant deeds shortly before the arrival of Christianity. Much of these stories have roots in actual historical events that are dated to the earliest medieval period of Ireland. And within the **Historical Cycle** is preserved an important collection of tales about Irish kings dating from the third century BC to Brian Boru around the year 1000 AD.

Did You Know?

"Once extremely popular on the British Isles, the Irish Wolfhound is an iconic dog breed of Ireland, and is highly valued and expensive. However, it almost completely disappeared from the British Isles at the beginning of the 18th century and considerable efforts were made for its

protection. However, thanks to the ban on the export of these dogs, but also thanks to the persistence of one Captain Darsley, this remarkable breed – one of the tallest in the world – has been protected in its native country. This breed is not only known for its hunting skills, but also for its attachment to man, its defensive character, and high intelligence. The Wolfhound – as the name suggests – is also a brave guard and a great fighter against wolves. The warlike Celts, the legend says, kept dogs of enormous size, using them in war and in the hunt. In Ireland, this dog became over time very popular, and in the Scandinavian countries it was used as a symbol of the nobility. Today, they remain one of the great animal symbols of Ireland."

The Mythological Cycle

Being the oldest one of all four cycles, and reaching into the oldest corners of the Irish history, the Mythological Cycle is the least well preserved of all, but nevertheless shows us a glimpse into a magical and mythical world and complex beliefs of the ancient Celts and their predecessors.

In it, there are no myths about the creation of the world. It is important to note that the Irish mythology does not begin with the creation of the world, but rather with the settlement of the island of Ireland. The most important sources are the so-called *Metrical Dindshenchas,* or "The Lore of Places" and also the well known *Lebor Gabála Érenn* or "The Book of Invasions". Many stories have been preserved, the most famous of which are The Dream of Aengus, The Wooing of Etain, and the stories of the first and second battles at Magh Tuireadh. One of the most beautiful Irish stories, The Tragedy of the Children of Lir, is also part of this cycle.

According to the myths, five consecutive waves of conquerors occupied Ireland. The first of these were the so-called Partholinians. The story of the Partholinians tells us that they were led by a hero known as Partholón, which gives them their name - *Muintir Partholóin* (People of Partholón). Together with his wife and their people, they sailed from the west and landed in the western province of Munster on the Beltaine. According to legend, they arrived onto the island some three hundred years after Noah's Flood, and introduced important new activities, such as farming, brewing, and building. The legend tells us that at the time, Ireland was already inhabited by a race of cruel, deformed beings known as the Fomorians, who represented the ancient, evil gods or pre-demons of Ireland. They fought the Partholinians, lost, and temporarily left Ireland going to the North Sea, from where they regularly returned to attack the new invaders. At the time of the Partholinians, the myth states that Ireland had only one plain, three lakes and nine rivers. During their stay, the Partholinians cleared four more plains and created seven more lakes. The first buildings in Ireland were also built at that time. However, the Partolonians all died of the plague, in a short amount of time.

The next story is that of the *Nemedians* and it tells us that they came from the west. The Fomorians returned from their northern islands to plunder the coasts of Ireland. The Nemedians won three battles against the Fomorians, but suffered heavy losses, and the plague broke out again, killing their leader Nemed. The Fomorians took advantage of the enemy's weakness and imposed a heavy tribute on them – two thirds of the grain, milk and children had to be given to them on each Samhain (Halloween). According to some legends, the Nemedians then perished to the last, and according to others, for fear of the plague and the return of the attackers, they broke up and left Ireland. From the survivors came the following two groups of conquerors, the Fir Bolg and the Tuatha de Dannan. Some 200 years after the departure of the Nemedians, Fir Bolg arrived at uninhabited Ireland. They divided Ireland into five counties: Connacht, Ulster, Leinster, Munster and Meath. Today, although Ireland consists of four provinces, the Irish word for province means "one fifth". Fir Bolg also established a kingdom. When the Tuatha de Dannan arrived, war broke out around the country. One legend claims that after the first battle of Magh Tuireadh, they established peace, and lived happily and contentedly for the rest of their lives.

The story of the *Tuatha Dé Danann* ("the folk of the goddess Danu") tells us that they sailed to Ireland in the fog from the sea and brought with them four great treasures - *Lia Fáil* (The Stone of Fal), the stone of destiny that stands today on Mount Tara and which would roar when the true King of Ireland stood upon it; then the *The Spear of Lugh,* a great and powerful fiery spear; *Claíomh Solais* (The Sword of Light), the deadly sword of Nuada; and a huge cauldron of the mighty god Dagda, which could feed all who ate from it. *Tuatha Dé Danann* meaning the people of the goddess Dana (the Great Mother Goddess whose name spread throughout Europe with the Celts - even the Danube was named after her), are described as demigods; they are a beautiful people, they know music and art. They are often associated with incredible magical powers and also with the building of the megalithic passage tombs that remain throughout Ireland today. Nuada, king of Tuatha Dé Danann, and Eochaid, leader of the Fir Bolg, fought in the first battle at Magh Tuireadh. The fight was fierce, and both sides suffered heavy losses. The Tuatha were defeated, but Nuada lost his hand in the fight and, by law, had to abdicate. The law said that "the king must not have physical defects of any kind." The Tuatha de Dannan elected a new king, Bres, who himself was a Fomorian, but it turned out that he was a bad king because he started raising taxes and taking tribute from his people.

It is written that Tuatha De Danaan have direct connections with the fairy creatures described in many of Ireland's myths. The connection is as follows: the people of Tuatha lost the land in the same way as the Fir Bolg people before them, defeated in the war against foreign invaders. Tuatha De Danaan and Ireland were attacked by a new group of people called the Sons of Miles (Milesians). After a long struggle against the invaders, the Tuatha were defeated and given a choice: either they will be exterminated, or they will go and settle in underground world. The god Dagda took them to the underworld where they were, according to one version of the legend, eventually turned into fairy beings.

The Tuatha Dé Danann are thought to have originated from the pre-Christian gods of Ireland, and Christian scribes, when writing down the legends, simply reduced them to historical kings and heroes. Tuatha Dé Danann came to Ireland from the four cities where they acquired occult skills and abilities - Falias, Gorias, Murias, and Finias. The story tells that they arrived in Ireland on dark clouds, although later versions, instead of the clouds, mention the smoke of ships that Tuatha Dé Danann burned to prevent their own retreat, determined to either win Ireland, or perish.

> *"It is God who suffered them, though He restrained them*
> *they landed with horror, with lofty deed,*
> *in their cloud of mighty combat of spectres,*
> *upon a mountain of Conmaicne of Connacht.*
> *Without distinction to discerning Ireland,*
> *Without ships, a ruthless course*
> *the truth was not known beneath the sky of stars,*
> *whether they were of heaven or of earth."*
> *– Lebor Gabála Érenn*

The first king of Tuatha Dé Danann was Nuada, also known as *Airgetlám* ("Silver hand"). Nuada led his people to war against the previous inhabitants of Ireland, the people of the Fir Bolg. In the last battle with the members of Fir Bolg, Nuada lost his arm fighting Sreng, a champion of Fir Bolg. Although they were outnumbered, Sreng and his three hundred warriors swore that they would fight to the last man. Nuada and Tuatha Dé Danann considered them noble warriors, and would thus not allow them to be exterminated. To that end they offered them a chance to keep a fifth of Ireland, in exchange for a truce. Nuada, however, lost his right to the throne as soon as he lost his hand because the ancient tradition of Tuatha Dé Danann dictated that a king who was physically challenged in any way (in this case, maimed), could not sit on the throne and be King.

Thus *Bres*, who was a semi-Fomorian, became the king of Tuatha Dé Danann. The Fomorians were a race of cruel giants, so King Bres made Tuatha Dé Danann pay a higher tribute to the Fomorians. As for the Fomorians themselves, there are conflicting legends about their appearance: according to one they were completely equal to humans, only larger, according to the other they had a body of a man and a goat's head, while a third says they were huge one-eyed, one-legged and one-armed monsters. All this time Nuada wanted to liberate his people from Bres' tyranny and regain the throne. Seven years later, the gods *Dian Cecht* and *Creidhne* magically replaced Nuada's severed arm with a silver one, and Nuada could become king again.

Dian Cecht, a major god who was a great physician and healer, made Nuada a powerful hand of silver, which had the power of movement in every finger and in the wrist, which meant that Nuada could regain the kingdom from Bres. Learning of this, Bres then set sail to meet *Balor of the Evil Eye*. Balor was the famed King of the Fomorians, a one-eyed giant, and agreed to gather an army against Nuada. But a Druid predicted to Balor that he would be killed by his own grandson. It turned out that this grandson was Lugh, son of Ethniu, daughter of Balor, and Ciana, son of Dian Cecht, the great healer. Lugh traveled to Tara to greet the High King Nuada of the Silver Hand. He was stopped at the gate, until he said he was a carpenter, but the porter said they had enough skilled carpenters in Tara. Lugh then said, *"I am also a blacksmith,"* but the guard still prevented him from entering. *"I am a warrior and a hero,"* Lugh said. *"Tara is well protected by her many warriors."* the guard replied. Lugh then replied, *"I am a scholar, a musician and a poet,"* but he could not enter yet. *"The news is that I know magic,"* Lugh said, but the guard did not move. Lugh finally asked him whether Tara had at least one man who knew all of these skills. Finally the guard opened the door for him, after Lugh states that he is a skilled smith, a hero, a bard, a wright, swordsman, and warrior. When Nuada heard of Lugh's arrival, he abdicated, realizing that Lugh's skills would finally rid them all of the Fomorians and lead them to freedom, and he became known as *Lugh Samildánach* ("skilled in many crafts") and gathered an army for the second battle of Magh Tuireadh. When the battle finally began, all the Tuatha who would have been killed were magically brought back to life. They defeated the Fomorians and killed their King Balor – as the prophecy told, Balor of the One Eye was killed by his own grandson, Lugh. Lugh defeated him with a sling, launching a precise shot directly into his eye, thus killing him. The life of the captured King Bres was spared, as he promised to share his knowledge of the right time for sowing and reaping. The bards of Tuatha de Dannan sang for centuries about the epic battles and skirmishes, until the arrival of a high and beautiful race of people from Iberia (Hispania), who were known as the sons of Miles, or the *Milesians*. It is likely that these were the bringers of the Celtic culture into Ireland.

A small digression about Dian Cecht: In Irish Mythology, he was a god of healers and blessed and healed the injured in a spring called *Tipra Sláine* ("well of healing"). Everyone who would bathe in it was instantly cured of all diseases and injuries - except, of course, decapitation. Dian Cecht had a son named Miach. Years later, Miach replaced Nuada's silver hand (made by Dian Cecht) with a new one, this one made of blood and flesh. His father, torn by jealousy, killed him. If any lesson can be learned from the myth, then it is this: if you are a god, never try to be better than your own father.

A few words about Lugh are needed as well – as he was one of the crucial figures in this cycle. As we said, Lugh was the grandson of Balor of the One-Eye, a cruel leader of the Fomorians and a powerful warrior. However, Lugh was not of the demonic look like the other Fomorians - he had his own appearance inherited from his mother, who was a human woman. Balor tried to kill him in his childhood because he learned of the prophecy according to which he would be killed by his own grandson. Lugh managed to escape and decided years later to join Nuada's army and Tuatha de Danaan. Lugh was not just a warrior, but also a blacksmith, a singer, a harpist, a historian and a magician, and a skilled craftsman as a whole. Overall, Lugh is a deity in the Irish Mythology, but can be considered as the type of hero-god. Historically, the figure of Lugh has many parallels in the wider Indo-European (and Old European as well) belief, and is likened to the many Sun deities across Europe, which are often youthful and heroic warriors. In Irish mythology, Lugh had several epithets by which he can be recognized. Some of these are *Lonnbéimnech* ("fierce striker"), *Ildánach* ("skilled in many arts"), *Conmac* ("hound-son"), and *Lámfada* ("of the long hand") – amongst others.

His cruel father, Balor, was the greatest Fomorian warrior, so powerful that it was said that his very sight could kill people. A giant in stature, Balor had one eye that could wreak havoc and destruction when it was opened, destroying entire armies with a gaze. Thus, Balor wore a steel visor over his eye that prevented him from killing his own army if he was to look at them. In battle, Balor would be brought before the enemy and his visor would be raised, exposing the enemy to his deadly gaze. In this way Balor killed Nuada in the second battle of Magh Tuieradh (Moytira) and nearly defeated the Tuatha. However, young Lugh stepped up to avenge Nuada's death, and confronted the monstrous Fomorian in the moment when the Tuatha De Danaan were ready to surrender. It was Lugh who defeated Balor in one fell swoop. In doing so, according to one legend, he used his magical fiery spear, while another says he used a slingshot. It is said that afterwards, as Lugh pierced Balor's skull, the power of his deadly eye was turned on the Fomorian army, decimating it. The Fomorians then surrendered and Lugh became the king of Tuatha De Dannan.

Did You Know?

"A shillelagh (saill éalaigh), is one of the iconic symbols of the Irish people, and a common part of the Irish folklore and mythology. A shillelagh is a unique walking stick that doubles as a club or a cudgel. It has a long stick body, and is topped with a rounded knob at its top. As such, it could quickly turn from a simple walking stick into a potent and formidable weapon. Shillelaghs were usually made from tough blackthorn sticks that were particularly knotty. And it was that knot that would become the head of the cudgel. To make the weapon more potent, some of the rowdier Irishmen would fill the knob with lead! Such a shillelagh was known as a "smachtín ceann luaidheh", or the "lead-headed cudgel". Over time, the shillelagh became associated with the Irish people, particularly abroad. Did you know that the officers of many of the Irish Regiments in the British Armed Forces carried carried shillelaghs as a defining feature of their uniform?"

And the story then brings us to one of Ireland's most famed mythical heroes, and one that is invaluable for the history of Ireland. Years after becoming King, Lugh had a son and named him *Sétanta* (Cú Chulainn). Cú Chulainn became a warrior just like his father was, and he used in battle a terrifying barbed spear called the *Gáe Bulg*. This horrific spear would tear the enemy's body when someone tried to pull it out. As in most legends, Cú Chulainn fell in love with a beautiful maiden, the noblewoman Emer. Emer's father *Forgall Manach* was not thrilled with the idea of his daughter marrying Cú Chulainn, and so he asked him to go and train with the famous warrior woman *Scáthach* in the land of Alba (Scotland). Forgall was hoping that the training would be too rigorous for the young warrior, and that it would in the end kill his daughter's suitor. Cú Chulainn went to *Scáthach*, and Forgall tried unsuccessfully to find a new husband for Emer in his absence. Everyone that was a potential suitor upon hearing that his rival was Cú Chulainn, gave up the proposition entirely. Cú Chulainn lived through the training, and upon his return, he asked for Emer's hand in marriage. Forgall Manach could not refuse him. Meanwhile, Ulster, where Cú

Chulainn decided to marry Emer, was ruled by Conchobar mac Nessa at the time. The king traditionally had the right to spend the first marital night with the wife of each of his subjects - and this is where a problem arose. Conchobar mac Nessa knew very well that if he gave up this right in Cú Chulainn's case, he would then lose all authority before his own subjects. On the other hand, he was afraid of what Cú Chulainn would do to him if he dishonored his wife. Still, a solution was found: King Conchobar would *sleep* with Emer on the night of her wedding, but the druid Cathbad, the king's adviser, slept between them and thus enabled the king to save his authority and also his head – without dishonoring Cú Chulainn.

"The first warp-spasm seized Cúchulainn, and made him into a monstrous thing, hideous and shapeless, unheard of. His shanks and his joints, every knuckle and angle and organ from head to foot, shook like a tree in the flood or a reed in the stream. His body made a furious twist inside his skin, so that his feet and shins switched to the rear and his heels and calves switched to the front... On his head the temple-sinews stretched to the nape of his neck, each mighty, immense, measureless knob as big as the head of a month-old child... he sucked one eye so deep into his head that a wild crane couldn't probe it onto his cheek out of the depths of his skull; the other eye fell out along his cheek. His mouth weirdly distorted: his cheek peeled back from his jaws until the gullet appeared, his lungs and his liver flapped in his mouth and throat, his lower jaw struck the upper a lion-killing blow, and fiery flakes large as a ram's fleece reached his mouth from his throat... The hair of his head twisted like the tangle of a red thornbush stuck in a gap; if a royal apple tree with all its kingly fruit were shaken above him, scarce an apple would reach the ground but each would be spiked on a bristle of his hair as it stood up on his scalp with rage." — Thomas Kinsella (translator), "The Táin"

Who Were The Milesians?

Tuatha Dé Danann remained the only inhabitants of Ireland until the arrival of the Milesians. The legend tells that they resided in what is today Spain (Iberian Peninsula), where one of their leaders, Breogán, founded the city of Brigantia and in it built a large tower. One day, while standing at the top of the tower, Breogán's son glimpsed a distant land across the sea. It is likely that Brigantia is the modern city of Corunna, on the very northern coast of Spain. It was known to the Romans as Brigantium. The tower in the myth could refer to the "Tower of Hercules", a 55 metres (180 ft) tall ancient lighthouse –

the oldest one in the world. It was built by the Romans in circa 1st century AD, but likely on the foundations of an even older, Phoenician lighthouse.

The glimpsed country across the sea was unknown to Breogán and his people and so they set out to investigate it. They landed on the west coast of Ireland, where they met the three kings of Tuatha Dé Danann: Mac Cuill, Mac Cecht, and Mac Gréine, a grandson of Dagda. They greeted the newcomers, but when they praised Ireland, the Tuatha were afraid that these men would conquer the country and so they killed the leader of their expedition, Íth – the son of Breogán. The Milesians then returned to Spain with his body and afterwards, his relatives, set sail to avenge him. When Amergin, the bard, and the druid of the Milesians disembarked, and met three great queens of the Tuatha who had prophesied to him that they would conquer the land, and he promised them that Ireland would bear the name of each of the three (one was called Ériu). The Tuatha kings demanded that the Milesians leave Ireland in peace for three days (a three-day truce). Amergin agreed to pull the ships at a distance of nine waves from the shore. After that, they would return and occupy the country. The Tuatha however, raised storms and fogs to prevent the Milesians from returning. Still, Amergin the Druid sang a magical ballad that dispelled the storms and the fog and the Milesians were able to disembark. Afterwards, the two groups agreed to divide the land between themselves. The division of the country was entrusted to Amergin.

The Ulster Cycle

This cycle is very close to the mythological cycle. Some of the characters reappear, and the same kind of magic is present once again. It is obvious here that the characters of the Irish mythology are not so much gods, but rather heroes who possess divine powers. The cycle consists of a group of heroic tales that tell the lives of Conchobar Mac Nessa, King of Ulster, the great hero Cú Chulainn, the son of the god Lugh, the warrior queen Medb of Connacht, along with their allies and enemies. The stories are about the births, growing up, training, battles, feasts and deaths of these heroes, and reflects a warrior society in which war consists mainly of duels, and wealth is measured by cattle. The stories are mostly written in prose. The central place is occupied by Táin Bó Cúailnge (The Cattle Raid of Cooley). Other important stories are included as well. The cycle develops around the hero Cú Chulainn and much more is learned here about his life and deeds. His real name was Setanta, but as a boy he killed a wicked guard dog that belonged to a man named Culann. This dog was as big as a horse and so fierce that it took three chains and three men on each chain to hold it. It tried to attack the boy, but the latter was too smart and killed it quickly. Culann, the owner of the dog, was inconsolable, so Setanta offered himself in place of the dog he had killed; so he got the name – Hound of Culann otherwise known as Cú Chulainn. The stories about Cú Chulainn and his works are exceptional. He was famous for his strength and courage. It was rumored that he owned 'Gae Bulg', the spear of Bulga, the god of thunder. Cú Chulainn died around 12 BC. Finally exhausted from the battle, he wanted to die standing. He equipped himself and tied himself to a stone pillar, but the enemies were afraid to approach him. Eventually a raven landed on his shoulder and started by pecking at his eyes - before long the great Cú Chulainn was dead. Cúchulainn remained a major force of Irish imagination and mythology. He is a symbol of unity and remembrance of a time when Ireland was free and proud.

The Fenian Cycle

The sagas of the Fenian cycle are based on the legendary Fionn Mac Cumhaill and Fianna - a group of elite warrior-hunters. They operated in units - groups of six warriors who were known as 'fiann', hence the name Fianna. The warrior bands protected the High King at Tara around the 3rd century AD. This cycle is sometimes called the Ossianic Cycle, because of many stories about Ossian, son of Fionn. Fianna were divided into the Baiscne clan, led by Fionn, and the Morna clan, led by his enemy, the Goll mac Morna. Goll killed Fionn's father, Cumhaill, in battle and Fionn was brought up in secret. As a young man, he learned the art of poetry and gained immense wisdom, when he accidentally burnt his thumb while frying the Salmon of Knowledge. After that, he could suck on his thumb and that made him wise in all areas. Numerous stories tell of his exploits. The two greatest stories of this cycle are *Tóraigheacht Dhiarmada agus Ghráinne* (The Pursuit of Diarmuid and Gráinne) and *Oisín in Tír na nÓg*. The story of Diarmaid and Grainna, which is one of the rare stories of the Fenian cycle written in prose, is a Celtic version of the famous story of Tristan and Isolde. This is a world of professional warriors who spend time hunting, fighting and embarking on various adventures in the world of magic. The new members of Fianna are expected to be knowledgeable in poetry, as well as to pass various physical tests and trials. Fionn represents King Arthur of Ireland, leading his warriors wisely in an endless battle against evil. Again, there are no religious elements here, unless it is respect for heroes.

The Historical Cycle

Part of the duty of the medieval Irish bards, or court poets, was to preserve the family history and genealogy of the king they served. This they did in poems that combined mythology and history to a greater or lesser degree. The resulting stories form the Historical Cycle, or the pre-cycles, as there are several independent groups. Tara, a hill in County Meath, was the center of ancient Ireland and the seat of kings from the earliest times to the 6th century. The meeting on Tara was held every 3 years, on Halloween. During this time all the kings met for six days. When the new king was elected, they held a feast, known as 'Terbfes'. A white bull would be killed and one of the druids would take its meat and drink the beef soup. He would then sleep while the other druids swarmed above him, and he would dream of a future king. When he woke up, they would interpret his dream and a new king would be elected. The kings in question can be completely mythological characters like Labraid Loinsech, who was the high king of Ireland around 431 BC, all the way to the completely historic Brian Boru. The most significant story of the Historical Cycle is Buile Shuibhne (Frenzy of Sweeney), which recounts the tale of Suibhne, king of Dal nAraide, who was cursed by St. Ronan and became half man, half bird, doomed to live in forests, fleeing from human society.

The Enigmatic Beings of Irish Folklore
Leprechaun
In Irish mythology and folklore, the leprechaun is a species of fairy creatures (faeries) inhabiting Ireland. Like the other fairies, the leprechaun is connected with the people of Tuatha Dé Danann, about whom we wrote above. Leprechauns and the stories about them can be found in the north of Ireland, in Carnlough, where, as legend has it, the local populace hunts them every first of August, and forces them to drink whiskey until they in turn force the winter to retreat. The leprechaun is usually depicted in the form of an elderly man dressed in a green suit. Leprechauns enjoy mischief, often shooting children with stones and riding on stray dogs. They are most commonly shoemakers by occupation, and are said to be very rich and bury their treasure during times of war. A typical leprechaun family has between two and nine members who have been drinking whiskey daily since they were little (five years old). According to legend, as long as you keep an eye on a Leprechaun, he can't escape, but as soon as you look away from him, even for a split second, the leprechaun will disappear. The best

way to prevent it from disappearing is to get him drunk with whiskey, which greatly diminishes his ability to disappear. Leprechauns very rarely appear in stories that deal with just them as the main characters. On the contrary, the leprechaun is usually just a supporting character in the story of the human hero. They are shown in most stories as more or less harmless creatures, or as grumpy creatures who enjoy mischief. In both cases they are considered as beings who are extremely rich and hide their gold in secret locations, most often in jars buried at the end of the rainbow. Over time, the leprechaun – an indivisible part of Irish folklore – has become a major symbol of the Irish culture and heritage, and remains so to this very day.

Clurichaun - (*clobhair-cean*) is a species of a fairy creature that resembles leprechauns to such an extent that some even describe clurichauns as a "nocturnal type" of a leprechaun. Unlike their green-clad cousins who only sometimes like to drink, the clurichauns are eternally drunk. Also they are both eternally frowning and are rude to others. It is said that they will - if you are good to them – protect your wine cellar, but if you mistreat them, chances are good that your wine will suddenly turn sour. It is also believed that clurichauns prefer most of all to come across a drunk person that lies in a ditch. They then perform various misdeeds over the drunk fellow.

The **Far Darrig** are another species of fairy creatures from Irish legends resembling a leprechaun. They are traditionally shown dressed in a red coat and red cap. Legends say that Far Darrig's mischief, unlike those of his cousin, can be very, very cruel. They are described as *"most sluttish, slouching, jeering, mischievous phantoms"*.

Dullahan remains one of the most spectacular creatures among the Irish fairy beings. It is believed that during certain Irish festivals, the Dullahan passes by in the form of a horseman in black. Dullahan is shown as a headless horseman carrying his head either on a saddle, or holding it in his right hand (following the example of this creature, a headless horseman from an American legend about Ichabod Crane is shown in Tim Burton's popular film "Sleepy Hollow"). The head itself looks like it is made of dough or moldy cheese, has a smooth surface with a disgusting smile and tiny black eyes. The whole head shines and it sometimes serves Dullahan for lighting the road. Everywhere this creature stops - one mortal dies. Dullahan also possesses supernatural vision, his head can see over the whole country, even in the darkest night, so it can also see the house of a person that is about to die, wherever the house is. People who see the Dullahan often go blind in one eye. Dullahan rides on a black stallion, using a human spine as a whip. But in some parts of Ireland Dullahan appears as a coachman on a black carriage drawn by six black horses. The carriage moves at such a high speed that the surrounding bushes can catch fire, and all the city gates open in front of the carriage, no matter how well they are bolted. Dullahan's head is allowed to speak only once during each journey, and even then he can only say the name of the person whose death he announces. Dullahan is considered to be the incarnation of the ancient Celtic god *Crom Dubh* who required human sacrifices every year to make the harvest a success.

Pooka - The Irish are not as afraid of any fairy creature as they are of pooka. Pooka moves across the country in the dark and can take several different shapes – being a shapeshifter. It most often appears in the form of slender black horse with sulphurous yellow eyes and a long mane that breaks down fences, scares livestock and destroys crops. Other manifestations include a small, deformed goblin, a tall, large, and extremely hairy humanoid or a black goat. Just the appearance of a pooka can cause hens to stop laying eggs and cows to stop giving milk. In some parts of Ireland, farmers often leave one row of grain unmown. This tradition is called "pooka's share" and derives from the belief that if one row of grain is left to him as a bribe, the pooka will not terrorize the farmer and his family.

Changeling - After the leprechaun, the most famous part of Irish folklore are the so-called "replaced children". According to legend, fairy creatures have problems with giving birth to offspring - offspring who are not born dead are horribly deformed. Adult fairy creatures find them repulsive and do not want them for their own. Therefore, they will often try to replace their deformed children with healthy human babies. The most common target are unbaptized children or those whom the family overly loves. In addition to its own deformed child, adult fairies will sometimes in the place of a kidnapped human child leave just a piece of wood. However, due to fairy magic, this wood would resemble a baby, or in some cases – an old and senile fairy.

The "replaced child" that the fairies left in place of the real one is never satisfied, except when some misfortune befalls any of the household members. Most of the time, the "child" cries and screams, his eyes are very dark, and his skin is usually yellow and to the touch feels like parchment. After just two weeks, the "baby" already has all the teeth, thin legs and deformed arms covered with light hair. A "child" such as that, brings misfortune to the household in which it is planted and is always hungry, and his only virtue is a talent for music. That is why these replaced children often show a talent for music that a human being would never be able to possess. These creatures do not live long, they rarely live to be ten years old. Most of them shrink and die in the first three years of life among the regular people. And adults can also be "replaced" by a fairy and are almost always arrogant and ruthless towards the family and friends. If the householders manage to drive the "child" out of the house, their real child will return to them unharmed. The best techniques for driving a fairy child away are fire, heat or forcing the "child" to reveal its true age.

Did You Know?

"The Celtic Harp is one of the easily recognizable national symbols of Ireland. With its elegance, beauty, and a majestic sound, this musical instrument could easily be likened to old Éirinn herself – that is, Ireland. During medieval Irish history, the instrument was a luxury, and was always associated with the Gaelic ruling class. As an instrument, it

required plenty of practice, skill, and deft fingers in order to be mastered, and was as such the prized feature of every royal court. Through time, the Celtic harp became a true symbol of Ireland. Did you know that a golden celtic harp on an azure background is the coat of arms of the modern Republic or Ireland? Throughout the centuries, a golden harp on a green background was the greatest symbol of Ireland."

Grogoch are another popular part of the Irish folklore. They look like little people, they are covered with thick red hair, they do not wear clothes, but are in places covered with twigs and leaves. According to legend, there are no female grogoch. They are completely resistant to heat and cold, and most often inhabit caves or hollows in rocks. Grogoch can become invisible and will only show themselves to certain people in whom they have trust. Sometimes it binds to individuals and helps them with sowing and reaping or in household chores, and after doing so it requires a special payment - a pitcher of cream. According to the stories, if the Grogoch's help around the house becomes a nuisance to the family, all that they should do is call a priest. Grogoch, like most other fairy creatures, are mortally afraid of the priest and will immediately flee the house in which the priest is present.

When talking about Irish folklore, one cannot overlook the **Banshee** - a female fairy creature that appears in three forms: as attractive young women, as older ladies, or as shriveled grandmothers. These three forms represent a triple aspect of the Celtic goddess of war and death (Badhbh, Macha and Mór-Ríoghain). A Banshee usually wears a grey cloak with a hood or a shroud, and is sometimes dressed as a washerwoman who washes the bloodstained clothes of the person whose death she wishes to announce. At night, with a piercing cry she announces the death of family members of noble Irish families such as the O'Neills, O'Briens, O'Connors, O'Gradys and Kavanaghs.

"...hence bean-síghe, plural mná-síghe, she-fairies or women-fairies, credulously supposed by the common people to be so affected to certain families that they are hears to sing mournful lamentations about their

houses by night, whenever any of the family labours under a sickness which is to end by death, but no families which are not of an ancient & noble Stock, are believed to be honoured with this fairy privilege."

Merrow is another important being from the Irish myth. The word merrow comes from the Irish words muir (sea) and oigh (virgin) and refers to females of these beings. Males are rarely seen, and they are often described as extremely ugly, covered in scales, with pig-faced features and long sharp teeth. On the other hand, the females are extremely beautiful and, as far as relationships with mortals are concerned, very promiscuous. Their feet are flat, and they have swimming webbing between their toes. They wear special clothes that help them travel through the sea currents: a small red cap with feathers, or a seal skin cloak. To get out on the mainland, the merrow must take off this coat. Every mortal who is there in that moment will gain complete control over the merrow which cannot be returned to sea until it gets its coat back. This way fishermen often try to get the merrow to marry them because it is considered that these beings are extremely rich because of the treasures from sunken ships that are common as their booty.

These are just some of the dozens of fairy creatures that inhabit Ireland's diverse and rich mythology and folklore. Of course, if we were to get into detail on all of these diverse creatures, and if we were to explore every nook and cranny of the expansive Irish mythology, we would have a lot more work on our hands, and we'd need many, many more pages to cover it all. This goes to show just how well preserved and rich this mythology is. Of course, this also tells us that successive waves of inhabitants of the island also left their cultural imprint. Plenty of what the Irish mythology consists of is certainly rooted in every successive stage of habitation in Ireland. With that being said, we need to remember that this still proves to be a big conundrum for researchers, as piecing together the puzzle of Ireland's early inhabitants still is a big challenge. However, some clues can be found in these four mythological cycles – could it tell us more about the peoples that make up the Irish genetic profile?

The story of the Milesians, for example, can provide some curious historical information – if it happens to have truth in it, of course. Could it be that the mythological Milesians, the sons of Míl, were the ones to arrive in Ireland and introduce them to the Celtic culture? While many modern scholars believe that this tale was a simple invention of the Christian writers, based on earlier legends, there can still be some considerable historical fact here. One of the major leads in this tale is of course, the fact that the Milesians were said to have come from Iberia, in modern Spain. The legend, as we wrote, tells of the people of Brigantium, who have glimpsed Ireland far away in the distance on the horizon. Brigantium is the modern day city of Corunna, in Spain's northern province of Galicia. The city itself lies on the coast, and is directly south of Ireland, as is Galicia on the whole. Galicia gets its name from an important Celtic tribe that inhabited it – the Gallaeci. These Celts could share their name with the Gauls of modern France, as well as the Gaels of the British Isles and Ireland. So, could it be – mythology aside – that the Celtic ancestors of the Irish sailed over from Galicia in Spain. The route towards Ireland would be clear and straightforward, and would follow a natural and logical expansion of the Celtic culture and peoples. Another major clue is the ancient name of Ireland – *Hibernia*. It is similar to the ancient name for Spain and its peninsula – Iberia/Hiberia. Some suggest that this name has roots in the Celtic language, coming from the name Iweriu (Fertile Land) (compare Old Irish Ériu, Modern Irish Éire). In the end, the clues are there for those keen to follow. And of course, history is never accidental – those that came to inhabit Ireland, even in the most ancient times, must have came from somewhere. As the centuries unfolded, and sailing became commonplace, we cannot disregard the fact that a new people – perhaps the Celts from Iberia – bumped into a fertile island in the North Atlantic, and decided that it was an ideal place for a new home. It's very likely that all those who came to "discover" or invade Ireland – except the Norsemen – were arriving from the southern route – from the direction of Iberia. Plenty of interesting research shows evidence of Neolithic seafarers, with established trade and travel networks across Europe. The latest research shows us that the earliest, Neolithic inhabitants of Ireland could have come from the Mediterranean, the Balkans, or Iberia. Plenty of DNA analysis on the human remains discovered in ancient megalithic passage tombs tells us that this theory might actually be possible. A good example is the so-called *Giant's Ring*, a late Neolithic henge monument located at Ballynahatty (*Baile na hÁite Tí*), near Belfast in County Down. This majestic earthwork henge and the passage tomb situated within it, yielded a curious discovery of the remains of a woman and four men. Recent DNA research revealed that the woman, and one of the men, belonged to the so-called *Early European Farmers*, i.e. those ancient settlers that migrated across Europe in the Neolithic. The DNA implied that the woman, whose remains were dated to 3343–3020 BC, *"shows predominant ancestry from early farmers"*, and *"haplotypic affinity with modern southern Mediterranean populations, such as the Sardinians"*. Further research confirmed that the woman shares the base genetics and visual characteristics of modern inhabitants of Spain and Sardinia. This, and other examples go to show that Ireland was "discovered" by maritime voyagers quite early on in world's history, and that it was probably *not* colonised from mainland Europe as previously thought, but from a southern route, across the Mediterranean and Iberia. With all these new and exciting discoveries, we can only eagerly await what new knowledge will float to the surface in the coming years.

So, it is actually more than likely that the four cycles of Irish mythology hold more historical fact – masked in legends and heroic tales – than it seems at first. The Tuatha De Danaan, the Fomorians, the Nemedians, the Partholonians and the Milesians – they could all very well be actual migrating tribes and peoples of Mainland Europe, settling in Ireland in successive waves. Either one could be identified with the Bell Beaker Folk of the Neolithic, with the Indo-Europeans, the Norsemen, or the Celts. And it is a crucial fact that these very peoples form the core of the Irish identity.

The myth of *Cú Chulainn* also shows some striking similarities with other Indo-European heroes and heroic tales. The bulk of these similarities are shared with the heroic tales of the pre-Islamic Persian hero Rostam, with the mythical events of the Germanic Lay of Hildebrand (for example, Cú Chulainn, Rostam, and Hildebrand all kill their sons unknowingly in their respective tales), and with the Greek epic hero Heracles. All of these curious similarities indicate a common, Indo-European origin. Similarities with the Greek hero Heracles are found in the episode where *Cú Chulainn* kills the hound with a club. Heracles likewise has to kill a ferocious hound – with a club – after being charged for stealing cattle. Some other, less crucial parallels with other Indo-European myths and deities include that of the Baltic Velnias or Slavic Veles – who are both seen as protectors of cattle, and also with Romulus, who is, much like *Cú Chulainn,* connected with a dog in his youth and surrounded by bands of young and heroic warriors. This serves as yet another reminder of just how powerful the Irish mythology is: powerful in a sense that it managed to preserve the parts of even its most ancient history and belief. When the history of Ireland as a whole is considered, this rich and venerable mythology comes to play a very important part – perhaps even more important than we think. It only remains to further immerse ourselves into this rich, enigmatic, and magical world, and to try and piece together this complex nend vast puzzle in order to find the traces of Europe's most ancient beliefs – hidden from sight in the tales of Irish mythology.

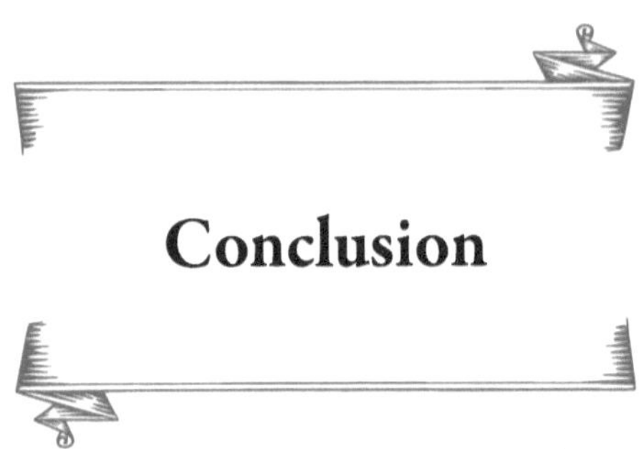

Conclusion

Ireland's fate was always dictated by the larger powers at play. As a lonesome rock in that fierce North Atlantic, the island of Ireland was ever left to be windswept and beaten by the winds of the centuries, struggling eternally for its rightful chance at peace and freedom. Alas, history is never linear – and seldom just. Ever since its earliest origins, this nation has been subjected to constant struggle. There is no doubt that the centuries were not kind towards Ireland and its folk. What's more, one could - without hesitation - say that old Erin Isle was ever at the brunt of history's harshest episodes. Nevertheless, it becomes clear that the Irish people managed to persevere even in the face of the toughest obstacles, preserving their identity all the while. Many of the world's nations could not say the same, having been long ago consigned to the dusty shelves of history. What made Ireland such a lucrative prize for so many a would-be conqueror? Undoubtedly, a lot of it has to do with Ireland's position - being situated so close to Britain, which in itself was always a target for new invaders, Ireland too was inevitably drawn into the larger events that swept up the British Isles. A good example are the Norse invasions. When the viking raiders and explorers chanced upon the rich lands of England, it wasn't long after that they landed on the shores of Ireland as well, precipitating a major chapter in its history. As an island nation, it was always an inevitable stop on the maritime journeys of many diverse peoples. The contacts with these peoples, whether hostile or peaceful, are exactly what shaped the Irish people into what they are today. From the Norse, the Norman's, the

English, the Celts, and all others - the route towards Ireland was inevitable at some point in history. Another factor is Ireland's lush climate and wealth of resources. In its early history, Ireland was heavily forested, and had plenty of wood to export. Ore was plentiful as well - ever since the Copper and Bronze ages, Ireland's mines were a rich source of ore. With the rise of agriculture, and by the start of the early middle ages, it was also becoming clear that Ireland had a great potential for cultivation and a rural economy. However, arguably one of the major contributing factors in Ireland's continual struggle was its lack of unity, and its major internal division. Still - at the time - clinging to their warlike and tribal Celtic heritage, the Irish failed to grasp the sense of a single, united people for far too long. Their separation into tribal, clan based kinships prevented them from effectively repulsing their invaders. Any conqueror of Ireland had their work cut out for them, as conquest was all the more easier when the Irish tribes and clans were divided and quick to wage war against one another. In the Iron Age, these were the many tribes that formed the foundations of later clans that established themselves, the major of these being the O'Neil, O'Donnell, Kavanagh, O'Connor, and numerous others. By the time the Vikings arrived, Ireland was split into numerous large and small kingdoms, with as many as 150 kings. Although they had one High King of Ireland, their divisions were at an all time high, and in many ways this was their downfall. Such divisions continued on throughout their history: with the arrival of the Normans, the Clans were divided in their support of the ruling class. Later on, with the arrival of the English, the people of Ireland were divided by their faith – Catholics and Protestants. Subtle ethnic differences also divided them – the Gaelic Irish and the Anglo-Irish were ever at odds. In modern times, Ireland was divided even more so – the Irish Civil War of the 1920's was the sad culmination of these differences. However, there can always be a positive conclusion – no matter how dramatic the tale is. In the case of Ireland, the centuries of difficulties nearly reduced it to ash – yet it rose up from those ashes like a true phoenix, rekindling the embers of its Gaelic heritage and identity, re-discovering itself all the while. Ireland of the 21st century is a land of prosperity and of pride. Its people have a clear definition of what it means to be Irish, and they hold on to their identity fiercely. One can say that the Irish have only – relatively – recently got a chance to breathe freely, and to explore their own identity without constraints from any "overseer". And that makes everything all the more exciting, filled with a sense of pride and belonging. The Irish are opening their eyes after centuries of slumber, and once more experiencing the magic of their Gaelic heritage, their Celtic culture, their myths and the tales from their history. They are preserving their unique Irish language, erasing the errors of the past, and once again standing firmly as a free and independent Republic of Ireland. And their story is still unfolding.

> *"To be Irish is to know that in the end the world will break your heart."*
>
> **— *Daniel Patrick Moynihan***

References:

Bradley, R. 2007. *The Prehistory of Britain and Ireland.* Cambridge University Press.

Brown, T. 2004. *Ireland: A Social and Cultural History, 1922-2001.* Harper Perennial.

Clare, A. 2011. *Unlikely Rebels: The Gifford Girls and the Fight for Irish Freedom.* Mercier Press Ltd.

Cooney, G. 2012. *Landscapes of Neolithic Ireland.* Routledge.

Curtis, E. 2012. *A History of Medieval Ireland: From 1086 to 1513.* Routledge.

Duffy, S. 1996. *Ireland in the Middle Ages.* Macmillan International Higher Education.

Dolan, J. P. 2010. *The Irish Americans: A History.* Bloomsbury Publishing USA.

Eaton, L. and McCaffrey, C. 2003. *In Search of Ancient Ireland: The Origins of the Irish from Neolithic Times to the Coming of the English*. Rowman & Littlefield.

Eogan, G. 2013. *Ireland in Prehistory*. Routledge.

Foster, R. F. 2001. *The Oxford History of Ireland*. Oxford University Press.

Fowler, C. and Cummings, V. 2015. *The Neolithic of the Irish Sea*. Oxbow Books.

Frame, R. 1998. *Ireland and Britain, 1170-1450*. A&C Black.

Fry, P. S. 1991. *A History of Ireland*. Psychology Press.

Haywood, J. 2004. *The Celts: Bronze Age to New Age*. Routledge.

Hollis, D. W. 2001. *The History of Ireland*. Greenwood Publishing Group.

Holman, K. 2012. *The Northern Conquest: Vikings in Britain and Ireland*. Andrews UK Limited.

Keating, G. and Keating, S. 1865. *General History of Ireland*. James Duffy.

Keating, G. 2009. *The History of Ireland*. Ex-Classics Project, Public Domain.

Kinealy, C. 2001. *The Great Irish Famine: Impact, Ideology, and Rebellion*. Macmillan International Higher Education.

Knirck, J. 2006. *Imagining Ireland's Independence: The Debates Over the Anglo-Irish Treaty of 1921*. Rowman & Littlefield.

Koch, J. 2006. *Celtic Culture: A-Celti*. ABC-CLIO.

Kostick, C. 2013. *Strongbow: The Norman Invasion of Ireland*. The O'Brien Press.

Lee, J. J. and Casey, M. 2007. *Making the Irish American: History and Heritage of the Irish in the United States*. NYU Press.

Mac Giolla Chriost, D. 2004. *The Irish Language in Ireland: From Goídel to Globalisation*. Routledge.

McGee, D. T. 1869. *A Popular History of Ireland: From the Earliest Period to the Emancipation of the Catholics [1829], Volumes 1-2.* Cameron and Ferguson.

McLaughlin, T. and Whitehouse, N. and Schulting, R. J. and McClatchie, M. and Barratt, P. 2016. *The Changing Face of Neolithic and Bronze Age Ireland: A Big Data Approach to the Settlement and Burial Records.* Journal of World Prehistory.

McNeill, T. E. 2005. *Castles in Ireland: Feudal Power in a Gaelic World.* Routledge.

Moore, T. 1882. *The History of Ireland: From the Earliest Kings of that Realm Down to Its Last Chief, Volume 1.* Longman, Brown.

O'Connor, T. P. 1886. *Gladstone, Parnell, and the Great Irish Struggle.* Edgewood Publishing Company.

O'Grady, S. 1881. *History of Ireland: Critical and Philosophical.* E. Ponsonby.

O'Kelly, M. 2001. *Early Ireland: An Introduction to Irish Prehistory.* Cambridge University Press.

Ó Néill, J. and O'Flynn, L. and Becker, K. 2008. *Iron Age Ireland: Finding an Invisible people.* The Heritage Council.

State, P. 2009. *A Brief History of Ireland.* Infobase Publishing.

Smyth, J. 2014. *Settlement in the Irish Neolithic: New discoveries at the edge of Europe.* Oxbow Books.

Sowell, T. 1981. *Ethnic America: A History.* Basic Books.

Williams, M. 2016. *Ireland's Immortals: A History of the Gods of Irish Myth.* Princeton University Press.

Walsh, O. 2002. *Ireland's Independence, 1880-1923.* Psychology Press.

Wrigth, T. 1849. *The History of Ireland, Volume 1.* John Tallis and Company.

The Black Death, 1348. EyeWitness to History. www.eyewitnesstohistory.com (2001).

Also by History Nerds

Celtic History

Ireland[1]

Irish Heroes

Grace O'Malley: The Pirate Queen of Ireland[2]

William Butler Yeats: Nobel Prize Winning Poet[3]

The Rise and Fall of Empires

Rome: The Rise and Fall[4]

The Sacrifice of a Generation

World War 1[5]

The Whirlwind of the Ages

World War 2[6]

Standalone

The History of the United Kingdom[7]

The History of Ireland[8]

The Napoleonic Wars: One Shot at Glory[9]

The History of America[10]

The Serbian Revolution: 1804-1835[11]

Stalin[12]

Peace Won by the Saber: The Crimean War, 1853-1856[13]

---

1. https://www.draft2digital.com/catalog/754037

2. https://www.draft2digital.com/catalog/680086

3. https://www.draft2digital.com/catalog/756184

4. https://www.draft2digital.com/catalog/591316

5. https://www.draft2digital.com/catalog/619671

6. https://www.draft2digital.com/catalog/635603

7. https://www.draft2digital.com/catalog/618976

8. https://www.draft2digital.com/catalog/631600

9. https://www.draft2digital.com/catalog/649544

10. https://www.draft2digital.com/catalog/654333

11. https://www.draft2digital.com/catalog/664621

12. https://www.draft2digital.com/catalog/820175

<u>The Fiery Maelstrom of Freedom</u>[14]
<u>The History of Scotland</u>[15]

---

13. https://www.draft2digital.com/catalog/824272

14. https://www.draft2digital.com/catalog/848656

15. https://www.draft2digital.com/catalog/865113

Also by Alastar MacTire

Celtic History

Ireland[16]

---

16. https://www.draft2digital.com/catalog/754037

Also by History Nerds

Celtic History
Ireland

Great Wars of the World
World War 1
World War 2
The Napoleonic Wars: One Shot at Glory
The Serbian Revolution: 1804-1835
Peace Won by the Saber: The Crimean War, 1853-1856
The Wars of the Roses

Irish Heroes
Grace O'Malley: The Pirate Queen of Ireland
William Butler Yeats: Nobel Prize Winning Poet
Scáthach
Finn McCool

The History of the Vikings

Vikings
Longships on Restless Seas

The Rise and Fall of Empires
Rome: The Rise and Fall

Standalone
The History of the United Kingdom
The History of Ireland
The History of America
Stalin
The Fiery Maelstrom of Freedom
The History of Scotland
Robert the Bruce
William Wallace: Scotland's Great Freedom Fighter
The History of Wales

Also by Alastar MacTire

Celtic History
Ireland